How to Overcome Embitterment With Wisdom

Christopher Arnold
Michael Linden

How to Overcome Embitterment With Wisdom

Library of Congress Cataloging in Publication information for the print version of this book is available via the Library of Congress Marc Database under the LC Control Number 2022937239

Library and Archives Canada Cataloguing in Publication
Title: How to overcome embitterment with wisdom / Christopher Arnold, Michael Linden.
Other titles: Ratgeber Verbitterung. English
Names: Arnold, Christopher (Christopher P.), author. | Linden, Michael, author.
Description: Translation of: Ratgeber Verbitterung: Informationen zum Umgang mit Verletzungen durch Ungerechtigkeit, Kränkung, Herabwürdigung und Vertrauensbruch. | Includes bibliographical references.
Identifiers: Canadiana (print) 2022023289X | Canadiana (ebook) 20220232970 | ISBN 9780889376137 (softcover) | ISBN 9781616766139 (PDF) | ISBN 9781613346136 (EPUB)
Subjects: LCSH: Adjustment disorders. | LCSH: Wisdom—Psychological aspects.
Classification: LCC RC455.4.S87 A76 2023 | DDC 152.4—dc23

The present volume is a translation of C. P. Arnold & M. Linden, Ratgeber Verbitterung: Informationen zum Umgang mit Verletzungen durch Ungerechtigkeit, Kränkung, Herabwürdigung und Vertrauensbruch, published under license from Hogrefe Verlag GmbH & Co. KG, Göttingen, Germany. © 2021 by Hogrefe Verlag GmbH & Co. KG.

© 2023 by Hogrefe Publishing
www.hogrefe.com

The authors and publisher have made every effort to ensure that the information contained in this text is in accord with the current state of scientific knowledge, recommendations, and practice at the time of publication. In spite of this diligence, errors cannot be completely excluded. Also, due to changing regulations and continuing research, information may become outdated at any point. The authors and publisher disclaim any responsibility for any consequences which may follow from the use of information presented in this book.

Registered trademarks are not noted specifically as such in this publication. The use of descriptive names, registered names, and trademarks does not imply, even in the absence of a specific statement, that such names are exempt from the relevant protective laws and regulations and therefore free for general use.

The cover image is an agency photo depicting models. Use of the photo on this publication does not imply any connection between the content of this publication and any person depicted in the cover image.

Cover image: © Kolbz – iStock.com

PUBLISHING OFFICES
USA: Hogrefe Publishing Corporation, 44 Merrimac St., Suite 207, Newburyport, MA 01950
Phone (978) 255 3700; E-mail customersupport@hogrefe.com
EUROPE: Hogrefe Publishing GmbH, Merkelstr. 3, 37085 Göttingen, Germany
Phone +49 551 99950-0, Fax +49 551 99950-111; E-mail publishing@hogrefe.com

SALES & DISTRIBUTION
USA: Hogrefe Publishing, Customer Services Department,
30 Amberwood Parkway, Ashland, OH 44805
Phone (800) 228-3749, Fax (419) 281-6883; E-mail customerservice@hogrefe.com
UK: Hogrefe Publishing, c/o Marston Book Services Ltd., 160 Eastern Ave., Milton Park, Abingdon, OX14 4SB
Phone +44 1235 465577, Fax +44 1235 465556; E-mail direct.orders@marston.co.uk
EUROPE: Hogrefe Publishing, Merkelstr. 3, 37085 Göttingen, Germany
Phone +49 551 99950-0, Fax +49 551 99950-111; E-mail publishing@hogrefe.com

OTHER OFFICES
CANADA: Hogrefe Publishing, 82 Laird Drive, East York, Ontario, M4G 3V1
SWITZERLAND: Hogrefe Publishing, Länggass-Strasse 76, 3012 Bern

No part of this book may be reproduced, stored in a retrieval system or transmitted, in any form or by any means, electronic, mechanical, photocopying, microfilming, recording or otherwise, without written permission from the publisher.

Printed and bound in the Czech Republic

ISBN 978-0-88937-613-7 (print) · ISBN 978-1-61676-613-9 (PDF) · ISBN 978-1-61334-613-6 (EPUB)
https://doi.org/10.1027/00613-000

Table of Contents

Preface		VII
1	**Embitterment – What Is It?**	1
1.1	How Does Embitterment Unveil Itself?	1
1.2	Why Is Embitterment so Agonizing?	3
1.2.1	Intrusive Memories	3
1.2.2	Withdrawing and Shutting Yourself off	4
1.2.3	Doing Things That Are not Effective and That Harm Yourself and Others	5
1.2.4	Disliking Yourself and Suffering From Yourself	6
1.2.5	Losing the Ability to Think Clearly	7
2	**What Offends People and Makes Them Embittered?**	11
2.1	Injustice	12
2.2	Ingratitude	13
2.3	Breach of Trust	15
2.4	Degradation	16
2.5	Violation of Central Values and Basic Beliefs	16
3	**When Does an Embittered Person Need Professional Help?**	21
3.1	Duration, Generalization, and Intensity	21
3.2	Self-Harm	21
3.3	Not Liking Yourself	22
3.4	What Can Be Done?	22
4	**Wisdom**	27
4.1	Wisdom as a Problem-Solving Capacity	27
4.2	Wisdom in Addressing Embitterment	28
4.3	Wisdom Skills in Problem Solving	30
4.4	Knowledge of Facts and Procedures – What Is Actually Going on?	31
4.5	Contextualization – Which Circumstances Play a Role Here?	33
4.6	Value Relativism – What Is It All About?	34
4.7	Change of Perspective – What Do Others Actually Think?	36
4.8	Emotional Empathy – How Do Others Actually Feel?	38
4.9	Self-Distance – How Do Others See Me?	39
4.10	Self-Relativization – How Important Am I?	40
4.11	Relativization of Problems and Aspirations – What Am I Actually Entitled to?	42

4.12	Emotional Awareness and Acceptance of Emotions – What Is Going on in My Heart? 43
4.13	Emotional Serenity and Humor – How Do I Keep Cool? 45
4.14	Long-Term Perspective – What Matters Is the Future. 47
4.15	Bringing the Past to a Close and Forgiving – Over Is Over 49
4.16	Uncertainty Tolerance – Accepting What the Future Will Bring 51
4.17	Difficult Problems and Simple Solutions 52
5	**What Is Psychotherapy?** 55
5.1	How Do I Find a Therapist?. 55
5.2	What Do Psychotherapists Do?. 56
6	**What Can Relatives Do?** 57
7	**Further Reading** 59
8	**Embitterment Checklist** 61
9	**Important Addresses** 63
Notes on Supplementary Materials. 65
Peer commentaries. 67

Preface

This book is intended to give a simple and at the same time professional introduction to the subject of *embitterment*. Everyone is familiar with embitterment, and many will have already experienced this feeling, just like other emotions such as satisfaction, joy, anxiety, and anger. This book describes what embitterment feels like, how it emerges, what the consequences are, what you can do about it, and what happens to make it pathological, so that you need professional help.

Embitterment is a reaction to injustice, insult, vilification, degradation, and breach of trust. Since ancient times, this emotion has repeatedly attracted attention. In literary fiction, many people and situations who suffer from embitterment and act out of this feeling have been described. One example is the character of Michael Kohlhaas, immortalized by Heinrich von Kleist in his 1810 novella. That account is based on a true story that happened in the 16th century. Hans Kohlhase was a merchant from whom two horses were stolen by a nobleman. Kohlhase demanded justice and filed a lawsuit, which was unsuccessful. His wife wanted to bring the matter to the sovereign. Instead of being heard, she was beaten to death. Thereupon Kohlhase equipped a small army and undertook a bloody campaign against all whom he considered complicit. He acted according to the motto "Let there be justice though the heavens fall!" During his search for vengeance, the cities of Wittenberg and Leipzig were set on fire, and tyranny spread. He finally attacked a silver transport of the Sovereign and sank the loot in the river Havel – because he did not want to get rich, but was seeking revenge. The district of Kohlhasenbrück in the southwest of Berlin was named after him. In the end, he was arrested and executed in Berlin. Kohlhase's story shows what can lead to embitterment and how bad the consequences can be.

Embitterment is not only an issue in fiction, but is also important in psychiatry, psychosomatics, and psychotherapy. It has been our experience in therapy that some affected people and relatives get relief when they realize that they are not the only ones who feel this way and that their condition is quite understandable. The suggestions described in this book have already helped some people with getting out of difficult situations and facing their problems successfully. Often relatives and friends also suffer from the embitterment of a loved one. It is hoped that this book will help with how to best act in such situations.

Since embitterment is an emotion that everyone knows and one that plays a role even in political discussions, understanding it can also help inform the public at large.

Christopher P. Arnold
Michael Linden

1
Embitterment – What Is It?

There is probably no one to whom one needs to explain what an insult and what embitterment are. In this respect, embitterment is nothing different from fear. You do not need a psychology textbook to understand such feelings. Many people can also remember situations when they felt embittered, just as most people can remember frightening situations. Everyone can also immediately see when someone else is embittered. Embitterment is a normal and common feeling.

Embitterment and fear have in common that they are "reactive" emotions: They are feelings that are triggered when something out of the ordinary has happened. In the case of fear, that will be a threatening situation, while embitterment is elicited by social stressors such as injustice, insult, vilification, degradation, and breach of trust.

1.1   How Does Embitterment Unveil Itself?

Research in psychology has shown that there are only a few basic emotions, from which many other emotional states can be put together. This is similar to colors: There are only a few basic colors but an infinite number of mixed colors. In this sense, embitterment is an emotion in which many emotional qualities flow together.

Imagine that you want to take the bus to an interview. You come to the bus stop and see that the bus has just left. You are disappointed and frustrated. But if you are on time yourself and the bus simply left a minute too early – that is, you should actually have caught the bus, then the bus driver is to blame, and what you feel will be anger. If, on the other hand, you were walking toward the bus stop while the bus was still there, and the driver drove off even though they saw you coming, that would lead to a response of wrath. If you could, you would like to punish the bus driver. And if the bus driver shows you their middle finger as they drive off, you feel attacked, insulted, and degraded. Resentment will arise, and in that situation, you will feel like you want to be aggressive and to strike back. You may even want to take a stone and throw it at the bus, despite the fact that that would probably not be a sensible act. If that was the last bus, and there is no longer any possibility of getting where you want to in time, then helplessness and despair will arise. If, on the other hand, all of this is actually irrelevant, and it does not make a significant difference whether you can catch the bus or not, these feelings will simmer in you for a short time and then the whole thing will fade away. You may no longer remember the incident after some time has passed. But when it comes to something important, things may look very different. Imagine that it was the bus that you should have taken to get to an interview in time. Now that you have missed the bus, you have also missed your chance to get a great job. That will be a mixture of frustration, anger, rage, resentment, and despair that will not go away so easily.

> **The Ladder to Embitterment**
>
> Something goes wrong (you miss the bus)
> → *Frustration*
>
> It did not have to happen (dawdling)
> → *Anger*
>
> Someone else could have acted differently (the bus driver could have waited)
> → *Wrath*
>
> Someone acted with intent – you were mocked or insulted (e.g., the bus driver laughs while driving away)
> → *Resentment and aggression*
>
> There is no alternative (there is no other bus or train connection)
> → *Helplessness and hopelessness*
>
> You could have set off earlier
> → *Self-reproach*
>
> It was very important (e.g., being late for an interview)
> → *Despair*
>
> **= Embitterment**

Self-reproaches are also painful: You should have left the house much earlier. You could have tried to get an earlier bus connection. It was the bus driver's fault; it was your own fault too. You are angry with oneself, with others, with the world. You experience yourself as a victim of unfairness and degradation. These are all nagging feelings. The bus driver did something that was unjust, and thoughts may arise regarding how to take revenge on the bus driver or on the bus company – perhaps by breaking the window of the bus stop. The feeling of vengeance is no longer linked to the rational attempt to solve a problem or undo something negative. It is only about the thought that "I'm going to treat you as badly as you treated me." Justice should be restored through compensatory injustice. Vengeance can be directed against the original culprit, but also against everything connected to them and sometimes even against someone who was completely uninvolved. You yourself have suffered something evil and therefore have an urgent desire to fight and do something bad to the world. At this point, embitterment becomes dysfunctional – that is, it leads to nothing good and under certain circumstances only makes everything worse.

Embitterment is a strong feeling. It can negatively impact every aspect of a person's experience. In the end, the person concerned suffers more from themselves and their feelings than from the consequences of the original incident. And unlike fear, feelings of embitterment are worse because the environment also suffers. Because the inner anger is ultimately directed against the world, those affected find it difficult to let others help them. One bathes in embitterment. If good advice is given – for example, to call the potential employer to tell him you are not coming and to ask for a new interview – then the reaction can be that the embittered person rejects this and says that everything makes no sense anyway. On top of that, showing disdain toward the other and insulting them, the embittered person tells them, "Direct your good advice somewhere else." Some of these aspects of embitterment are described in more detail below.

1.2 Why Is Embitterment so Agonizing?

1.2.1 Intrusive Memories

One of the characteristics of the human memory is that it tends to remember negative more than positive things. Negative memories create a higher level of emotional involvement than positive ones do. Nobody gets upset about it, or would remember it any longer, if they ran down the stairs uninjured in the morning. However, falling down the stairs in the morning will possibly be remembered for a lifetime. Most of all, we remember what has an emotional meaning, especially when something bad has happened to us. That sticks in our memory. Even if you actively try not to think about it anymore, the memory will keep imposing itself. In psychology, this is referred to as an *intrusion*. However, you can also be reminded again and again through external stimuli – for example, in the case described in the previous section, when you see a bus, or in the case described here, a staircase. The more important the event was, the less you are able to forget it. This means that those affected get stuck in the past.

The bad thing is that the memory is linked to the original feeling. If you think of a situation in which you have been successful, you feel satisfaction and joy. If you think about the missed bus or falling down the stairs, then you probably feel tension. In this way, the memory of the original event becomes the trigger for further feelings of embitterment. You remember how you were insulted or betrayed and immediately you feel hurt and embittered. Those affected not only suffer from what has been done to them that developed in a negative way as a result, but they also suffer much more from having to remember the triggering event and the painful emotions associated with it.

Thus, a vicious circle develops. Memories trigger embitterment. These negative emotions themselves lead to the memory becoming more and more powerful emotionally. That means that emotions and the associated memories become more frequent. This prevents the triggering event from being properly processed psychologically. The triggering situation cannot be forgotten for months or years later and remains stressful. In the end, the real problem is no longer the incident in the past, but the intrusive memories that arise in the present.

Since the thoughts are uncomfortable, people experiencing this cycle also develop a kind of fear of these memories. They do not want to remember and feel frustrated and in a bad mood when they do. Therefore, they often try to suppress the thoughts. But you can not forget important things. Try to forget the name of your boss if you have an argument with them. Trying not to think about something leads to the frequency of the memory increasing and being perceived even more intensely. Thus the thoughts and the attempt to forget about them amplify each other. You are in a vicious circle.

If you want to get rid of embitterment, you have to learn to remember without getting upset. This can be quite similar to how, for example, everyone happily pokes fun at a former math teacher at a class reunion – someone who, at the time certainly spread fear, horror, and sense of disparagement.

1.2.2 Withdrawing and Shutting Yourself off

As already mentioned, memories and emotions involved in embitterment are also triggered by external circumstances, such as signs, logos, places, or conversations about the triggering event. This can lead to avoidance of such situations or people. If the problem has happened in connection with an employer, for example, it can be that the workplace is avoided. However, this does not only have to concern the location of the event, as other places that are linked to the triggering event may also be avoided. If the critical life event occurred in a certain supermarket, for example, then not only this market but other branches or even the street is avoided because you might meet former customers. If the situation happened in a group of friends, the embittered person may avoid acquaintances and withdraw themselves more and more. This is understandable, because it is about pushing away stimuli and situations in order to not have to feel the negative emotions. However, this only adds to the problem, and the thoughts pile up. Unfortunately, the basic psychological principle applies that everything will only get worse if you avoid it.

Embitterment also leads to withdrawing from interests, hobbies, and other activities. Anyone who is embittered feels bad and experiences everything around them negatively. You do not go to the cinema, you do not meet other people, and you do not feel like pursuing hobbies when you feel bad. Besides, you do not care about anything. This means there is another vicious circle. A bad mood leads to withdrawal and retreat and an impoverishment of life. There are no more distractions, and no more joys, which will lead to a deterioration in your mood even more.

When help is offered by friends and family, those affected usually feel offended. Needing help inevitably means having a problem. But why should the person affected change something when the problems only lie with others? If the partner feels the pressure of suffering and advises the embittered person to seek therapeutic help, this is often felt to be offensive. This can lead to the person turning away from loved ones, refusing any help and even rejecting it with embitterment, which worsens the symptoms and ends up again in a vicious circle.

If you want to get rid of embitterment, you have to keep in contact with other people, you must not close off and withdraw into yourself, and above all not bite the hand that wants to help you.

1.2.3 Doing Things That Are not Effective and That Harm Yourself and Others

Avoiding places and people makes many problems even worse. If someone withdraws from work or reacts disgruntledly to colleagues and superiors, further conflicts may arise. A reduction in work productivity and, in extreme cases, unemployment and financial problems may follow.

A lawyer reported that two neighbors quarreled because the fence between their properties went 10 cm (roughly 4 inches) beyond the property line on one side. The result was a conflict that continued to escalate and ultimately resulted in lengthy and costly legal battles. Nobody could give in. They could easily have "leased" that bit of land for a good case of wine. We see this again and again: that people with embitterment try to restore "justice" through legal means. In the end, the legal battle costs more than the original damage caused. Some legal disputes even end up in the higher courts.

Also common are embittered custody battles, where no one can let go, and the child who is said to be so loved is seriously damaged. In the end, it is no longer a question of finding a solution to the problem, but of harming the other as much as possible in order to leave the stage as the "winner."

Being reprimanded by the boss in front of colleagues can trigger embitterment, but you only harm yourself if you do not let the whole thing rest. Some of those affected drive themselves into financial ruin as a result of legal disputes, as the costs for the lawyer and other expenses add up over time. Those affected also harm their environment. They are using up savings for a futile legal battle and interpersonal relationships fall apart. Spouses, relatives, and friends also suffer from revenge fantasies, and aggressive and depressed mood, and loss of interest. They experience themself to be helpless and are offended by the reaction of the person concerned and therefore withdraw into themselves as well.

Most people will have seen that parents sometimes forbid a child from going to an amusement park with friends. If the reaction is embitterment, the child may say, "I do not want to go anymore," when the parents offer to go with the child on the weekend. Instead of joyfully seizing this opportunity, the child cuts off their nose to spite their face. They not only miss going to the amusement park, but also the chance to enjoy the benefit of the parents being particularly generous on that day.

Many people have also experienced having a good reason to be angry and embittered with their partner – for example, because they have been criticized in the presence of others. The partner apologizes, saying they did not mean what they said, and they offer to make amends. Instead of this chance not only for reconciliation, but also to be treated to a meal at an expensive restaurant, their answer is often a harsh rebuff that is ultimately not very helpful. Sometimes, we realize we are doing something stupid, and yet can not stop ourselves, but are carried away by our feelings. At the end of the day, one is mad at oneself.

> **Tipp**
>
> If you want to get rid of embitterment, you should weigh the benefits and costs.

1.2.4 Disliking Yourself and Suffering From Yourself

As the last example illustrates, embittered people can not only suffer from what has happened, but above all from themselves. An embittered person is caught in a variety of negative feelings. The basic mood is dysphoric, aggressive, desperate, and irritable. If the critical event comes up, there are outbursts of emotions. The behavior often no longer matches the "normal" behavior of the person. When they are reminded of the event, they can appear to be someone completely different from who they normally are.

Embitterment is not a pleasant feeling. Aggression and anger do not stop themselves. Feeling guilty about yourself can lead to self-blame. You ask yourself, How could you not have been more careful? How could you allow something like this to happen at all?

In addition, the embittered person often blames the world as a whole. People usually expect good things to happen to "good people," and the "bad" people to be punished. A critical life event that you consider to be not fair can lead to a loss of faith in the world and in justice itself. The just world, which is expected to guarantee that good people are rewarded, turns into an unpredictable and punishing place. The embittered person often feels helpless and at the mercy of life.

Helplessness is an emotion that is often observed in connection with embitterment, not least because the critical life event itself is often irreversible. The fact that the spouse cheated cannot be undone. This can also put the person in a helpless, desperate state. If you cannot do anything about something and still have to deal with it mentally, especially if this takes place over a longer period of time, it can affect your overall life satisfaction.

If we want to get rid of embitterment, we need to realize that it means recognizing that "I" lose my temper and "I" work myself up. So one should ask oneself, why am "I" doing this to myself, as it makes no sense to harm oneself?

1.2.5 Losing the Ability to Think Clearly

Psychology research has shown that the interpretation of a situation with attributions and automatic thoughts determines how people react. Those who regard the examination grade "B" as a great result will be happy. Whoever only sees the missed "A" instead, will react with disappointment and be unhappy. The reverse is also true. Emotions determine what we think. If you are in an argument with your partner and you are disappointed, you will primarily see their negative sides. You will only remember past conflicts, only see the mess in the house, and respond to what are actually irrelevant comments with sharp counterarguments.

In such cases, there are also typical thought patterns of offended and embittered people, driven by their emotional state. Experiences of injustice or breach of trust are often irreversible. There is no magical way of turning back time so the whole thing never happened. If you are hurt, you want justice in spite of everything. The damage suffered, be it the loss of money, a job, or custody of the children, is often irreversible. What the other person said can no longer be undone.

This often creates a desire for revenge in embittered people. They demand compensatory justice for all that has been done to them. In compensation, something bad should also happen to the other person. The injustice should be compensated for by revenge against the person. Many offended and embittered people see themselves as victims of the situation, who now have the right to justice. Reparation for the damage is demanded.

The combination of anger, aggression, and the need for retribution often gives the embittered person excessive thoughts of revenge: Whoever did this to them should pay for it. Let them be sorry for what they did. Thinking that the company of the boss who fired you will go bankrupt and that the boss is now unemployed can make you smile. To imagine something bad happening to a "bad" person gives you a sense of satisfaction, especially when it comes to your own tormentor. These are normal human thought processes, as almost everyone has experienced them. Thoughts of revenge are normal in such a state. It is human to react to a negative life event in this way. Almost everyone has caught themselves imagining that something bad also happens to a person after they hurt someone else. The fantasy of running a car over the culprit or seeing them fall and hurt themself can create a feeling of satisfaction.

Experiencing such thoughts can be shocking. It can be surprising that you suddenly imagine doing something bad to your tormentor, such as running your car over them. It can be surprising to suddenly have these thoughts in your head, when you normally see yourself as a peaceful person, and such trains of thought normally seem completely unacceptable. Yet such thoughts arise and are perfectly human. A thought is not the same as reality.

This becomes a problem when plans change to intentions to act out such thoughts. When those affected start to think about how to set fire to their old workplace, stab the tires of their neighbors, or even kill their ex-partner, and when they start to develop concrete plans for this, then danger is pending. Now, at the very least, the person should realize that they are in a critical condition and need help as soon as possible.

The feeling of helplessness can also lead to thoughts of suicide. In the worst cases of embitterment, the insult can trigger so much psychological stress that the person sees no other way out other than to kill themself. In combination with fantasies of revenge, in the most extreme cases, thoughts and actions of an "extended suicide" – that is, a suicide after killing the other person – can occur. In their desperation and vindictiveness, they see no other option but to kill themselves and their tormentors.

> **Tipp**
>
> If you want to get rid of embitterment, you should realize that revenge may feel sweet, but it is a sweet poison.

2
What Offends People and Makes Them Embittered?

Disagreements and arguments arise in contacts with other people. The boss who makes inappropriate comments, the acquaintance who is always late for appointments, and the partner who always puts the toothpaste tube in the wrong place, are some common examples. These everyday disagreements between people are irritating, annoying, and frustrating. There is also a lot of stress in life, such as work overloads, noise, and illness. However, *social stressors* such as insult, degradation, breach of trust, or injustice are particularly stressful. They hit hard, they hurt, and they can trigger embitterment.

> **In the Beginning There Was Embitterment: The Story of Cain and Abel**
>
> (Gen 4:1–16)
>
> "Abel became a shepherd, while Cain was a farmer. One day Cain offered some of the harvest as an offering to Jehovah. Abel offered some of his firstborn lambs from his herd along with their fat. Jehovah looked benevolently upon Abel and his offering. However, he did not look upon Cain and his offering with benevolence. Cain was very angry. After that, Cain said to his brother Abel: "Let us go out to the field." When they were in the field, Cain rose against his brother and killed him."
>
> This story shows that Cain felt he had been treated unfairly and was so angry or embittered about it that he even killed his innocent brother. He believed that justice requires that God treat him and his brother equally (comparative justice). In this case, that would have meant that God would also have accepted his sacrifice if he accepts his brother's benevolently.
>
> Several things can be deduced from the story:
> - Embitterment is as old as humanity.
> - Embitterment is triggered when someone feels that they have been treated unfairly.
> - Obviously, what is unjust is not easy to determine. Can one force a gift of food on God, and does God not have the right to decide for himself what he wants (right to self-determination)?
> - Embitterment can lead to very dysfunctional consequences.

2.1 Injustice

The issue of justice has since ever been a topic for mankind. Socrates, Plato, and Aristotle tried to define the term. Aristotle describes justice as a morally valuable and desirable virtue. He sees someone as unjust who breaks the law, or insatiably wants more than he deserves, or acts unequally.

Humans have a largely innate understanding of justice. This basic assumption has been extensively researched in psychology under the heading of *belief in a just world* psychology. Its central findings are that people:
1. tend to expect justice from those around them;
2. believe that everyone gets what they deserve;
3. believe that they can control positive or negative events through appropriate behavior; and
4. assess themselves as fair.

Humans want the world to be just – that is, at least to treat them fairly. When we are convinced that the world is fair, it becomes predictable and controllable, and one feels safe. If something good happens to us, it is only the "logical" consequence of the good deeds that we have previously done. If something bad happens to another unpleasant person, we assume that it happens because of their bad character. "Bad things should happen to bad people," as the saying goes. This gives meaning to what happens to oneself and other people. The fact that positive and negative events are often involuntary, random, and hardly controllable is ignored.

However, in psychological research, the belief in a just world is described as a "fundamental delusion." Life is full of injustices that everyone must face. We encounter these injustices almost every day – be it at work (e.g., through discrimination by one's boss) or at home when it comes to the distribution of household tasks. These do not necessarily have to be huge injustices, because even small hassles that do not correspond to our understanding of justice can offend and embitter us. The following little case history from Mr. B. and Ms. M. should help to make the problem a little more tangible:

> **Case Example 1: Injustice**
>
> Mr. B. and his former girlfriend, Ms. M., have recently separated. The separation went without any major problems. There is still, however, a bank account with 100 dollars in it.
>
> Mr. B. believes that this money must be divided equally, as both have made deposits into the account to cover joint expenses. Since the account is in the

name of Ms. M., however, she feels that the money belongs to her. She has sole power of disposition. But Mr. B. feels that Ms. M.'s approach is unjust. He is outraged because he feels betrayed.

In the coming days, Mr. B. tries hard to get the 50 dollars that he thinks he is entitled to. However, the conversations with Ms. M. are unsuccessful. He tries again and again to reach Ms. M. and gets in a bad mood when he thinks about the incident. The longer the matter drags on, the more annoyed he becomes.

And all that for 50 dollars, he will otherwise spend en passant.

Mr. B. experiences injustice in this example. One might wonder why Mr. B. wastes so much energy on such a small amount of money and suffers from a seemingly absurd trifle. The answer lies in the violation of core values. Mr. B.'s sense of justice requires that the money that is in a "joint" account should be divided equally in the event of a separation, regardless of who the account is legally registered to. This central assumption was violated by Ms. M. She uses her power of disposal to the disadvantage of Mr. B. and keeps the money. It was therefore the behavior of Ms. M. and not the amount of money itself that leads to Mr. B.'s extreme reaction. It does not matter that the trigger is a very small, almost irrelevant amount of money. An everyday situation, such as the loss of a small amount of money, deeply affects Mr. B. He could have dropped the same amount of money on the street, and his reaction would have been completely different. The decisive factor in insult and embitterment reactions is not the object, but the violation of the person's values.

2.2 Ingratitude

Gratitude is important to many people, because gratitude also means receiving attention and recognition for what you have done. Doing something for others and receiving thanks from the other person is an outcome that is connected with kindness. After a generous action, people like it when other people show themselves to be grateful. This does not have to be limited to something material. Even a simple "thank you" is seen as appreciation. But it also has something to do with compensating you for your own efforts. If I have done something for someone without, for example, receiving a fixed fee or payment, then a note of gratitude is a substitute for material compensation. Gratitude not only includes a kind word, but also behavior. When I accept a parcel for a neighbor, I expect a thank you. However, I also expect the neighbor to accept a parcel for me when the opportunity arises. In this respect, gratitude also has something to do with justice. Ultimately, it is about a balance on a material or, even more, a psychological level.

If you show ingratitude rather than gratitude, this can also trigger a sense of insult and a feeling of embitterment. Once again, ingratitude is a violation of the central assumption of justice. If someone does not thank you and does not prove to be grateful, then this triggers a defensive reaction, reproach, and aggression. You will not do that person another favor, even if they should need it. The following case study may help to illustrate this.

> **Case Example 2: Ingratitude**
>
> Ms. C. is a secretary in a medium-sized company. She cares for her boss, Mr. D. She makes phone calls and prepares meetings for him and supports him however she can. It was her dream job to this day and she enjoys what she does.
>
> In the past few months, there has been considerably more work, due to the dismissal of a colleague. Ms. C. has worked a lot of overtime without a single complaint. Since she has mastered her job and is efficient, she can do this and keep everything going.
>
> However, she would have expected that her boss would notice and acknowledge it with a word of appreciation. Nothing like that happened. Mr. D. accepts the additional service without comment, as if it were a matter of course. She has saved the department from total chaos. "Without me, everything would have gone down the drain here!"
>
> While there used to be nice and friendly communication between her and her boss, she now reacts with a feeling of hurt, with grumpiness, and also derives a certain satisfaction when she lets her boss down.

Triggered by the ungrateful behavior of the superior, Ms. C. feels disrespected, not appreciated, and offended by his ingratitude. For Ms. C., it is incomprehensible that her boss does not see and appreciate her commitment at all, takes it for granted, and does not even give her a word of appreciation or thanks. That would not have cost him much. As a result of the ingratitude, the entire work situation for Ms. C. has changed significantly. Her good relationship with her boss is severely disturbed, her work enthusiasm is reduced, and there are even feelings of a desire for revenge, if not acts of revenge, in that she no longer does every task given to her and no longer cares for him as before.

2.3 Breach of Trust

The phrase "trust is good, but control is better" is well-known. Still, things do not work without trust. Anyone who thinks they have to control their partner to ensure that they are not cheating on them will destroy the relationship. This is precisely why a breach of trust is so hurtful. You trust your spouse, children, coworkers, and friends, in the expectation that they will not betray you and that they will not inappropriately take advantage of you. Trust goes hand in hand with uncertainty because the behavior of other people can never be fully controlled. Trust means giving up control, giving freedom to others, and surrendering to other people to a certain extent. In this respect, trust makes you vulnerable and fragile. If the other person abuses the trust placed in them, and a breach of trust occurs, this leads to negative feelings such as disappointment, reproach, anger, despair, or embitterment.

A breach of trust can be very damaging to a relationship. A well-known example of a breach of trust is cheating in a love relationship. Partners trust each other; they have to trust each other! If a partner breaks the rules, it can lead to feeling seriously hurt and also end in embitterment.

> **Case Example 3: Breach of Trust**
>
> After Mrs. E. married her husband, the couple had two children. Her husband focused on his career. Mrs. E. put her career in the background. She supported her husband in his professional advancement, helped him in any way possible, and gave him all the freedom to pursue his career. She took care of the children, his parents, the house, their friends, and was always at his side for business duties.
>
> Their marriage was close and harmonious for 15 years. Then Mrs. E. happened to find a very emotional letter from her husband to a work colleague, from which it emerged that he had started a sexual relationship with this (significantly younger) woman behind her back a long time ago and that he felt a close relationship of trust with her.
>
> For Mrs. E., "the world collapsed" at this moment. She was bitterly disappointed, hurt, and outraged by how her husband could betray her marriage and inflict such a humiliation on her ("after all that I have done for him and our family"). She ponders and blames herself for not having noticed anything for so long and how she could have been "such a stupid cow," trusting him and doing everything for him over the years. It was so unfair.
>
> Mrs. E. has been full of resentment, embitterment, and despair ever since. She remembered sitting with him trustfully in the living room, while at the same time he already had a sexual affair with the other woman. She can not forgive her husband for betraying her like that. Out of revenge, she starts a "tough divorce war" and does not care that the children suffer from it.

2.4 Degradation

"Dignity" is a term that one encounters in many different contexts. Constitutional laws, such as the German basic law, claim that "the dignity of men is unimpeachable." Historically, the word "dignity" is related to value. It describes the appreciation of a person and, last but not least, their position in the community. To respect the dignity of a person means to appreciate and respect them.

If one's dignity is not respected, it means that one is not valued by the other. You are, so to speak, worth less than other people. This is especially true in the case of *degradation* (related terms are humiliation, loss of pride, abasement, mortification, and discrediting). Degradation is an insult.

> **Case Example 4: Humiliation**
>
> Mr. G. is a manager in a large company and fully committed to his work. He is also very proud of what he has achieved. The company's sales are impressive. However, there are problems with a particular project. Mr. G. is well aware of this and is doing everything possible to improve the situation. In a conference with other managers, he also reports on the difficulties and what is further planned.
>
> His head of department takes the opportunity to speak and warns that financial losses are imminent. But then he also blames Mr. G. personally in the presence of his colleagues. Mr. G., he says, should have realized earlier that things were going in the wrong direction. Such a thing would not have happened to a "real" manager. He is probably not properly qualified for his job and his salary.
>
> Mr. G. is speechless and at a loss. After the meeting, he leaves the room and can not stop trembling. As a result, he takes sick leave and ponders how he can harm the company and make his boss suffer.

This short example shows how one word may be enough to upset a person. In the present case, this was the reference to a "real" manager who would have solved the problem early on. Mr. G. feels degraded by this one word. It is an attack on his self-worth, vilifying him, and ultimately also unjustly disgracing him. This sort of defamation of oneself, of one's values or actions, can lead to pronounced embitterment.

2.5 Violation of Central Values and Basic Beliefs

Everyone has an idea of how the world should work and what is good and right. Such *worldviews* or *basic beliefs* are partly innate, such as the already-mentioned belief in justice. Others are innate and instilled at the same time, such as the question of whether a partnership should last. Others are purely cultural, such as the belief that it is right or wrong to eat pork. This is similar to language. Language competence is innate in all people. The dialect is what is learned.

Such beliefs involve very powerful psychology. They serve to ensure that we behave coherently across our lifespan. Anyone who believes that hard work and thrift are important virtues will save money all their life, and finally be able to build a house. The central beliefs of a person help them to have confidence in the world, in others, and in themself. They help people to decide what is important and what is not, who we trust according to our values, or who we prefer to avoid. Once basic beliefs have been acquired, they help us to shape the world according to these norms. Muslims are building mosques and Christians churches, irrespective of the traditions of the countries where they are living. Americans prefer to eat steaks with knife and fork, Chinese to eat glas noodles with chop sticks. Basic beliefs define culture. One applies one's values every day. We rarely question our own values. As long as the world as a whole and other people adhere to these values, we have a good feeling about them. If someone else does not follow our rules this leads to irritation and rejection, if not aggression.

Since basic beliefs control our behavior over the entire lifespan, they are largely resistant to change. To understand this better, the comparison with language may be helpful here. Once you have learned a mother tongue by the age of 20, you will never get rid of it. At that point, you can no longer learn a (second) mother tongue, but only foreign languages with at best rough fluency. Those who consider honesty to be a valuable asset will probably not engage in stealing throughout their life, even if things are lying around openly in a department store.

Basic beliefs and values also determine transgenerational behavior. Parents tell their children that they are American or Canadian. This is internalized from the age of 10. Even if you live abroad for decades, you remain an American or Canadian. Thus, basic beliefs are also state-forming concepts. They create cohesion between a large number of people. They identify a group and, of course, differentiate them from others. Having the same values and worldviews gives people a feeling of belonging to their culture. When Mexican and American soccer teams are in contest, Mexicans will typically support the Mexican team, even if they live in the US for long.

As these examples show, basic beliefs are very stable. Much more significant, however, is that people tend to defend their basic beliefs and thus their self-definition when those are attacked. If a Mexican makes derogatory comments about Dallas in the presence of a Texan, the usual reaction is that this is experienced as an attack and answered with counteraggression – that is, Dallas is defended and Mexico City is made out to be bad. This leads to resistance whenever the basic beliefs, worldviews, and basic values of a person are questioned. On TV talk shows, you can observe how otherwise well-behaved people suddenly become loud and aggressive, do not allow the other to finish speaking, and defend their own political or ideological positions "bitterly," when these are questioned. Many wars around the globe are ultimately worldview-based, ideological, national, or religious battles that are fought regardless of the number of casualties they lead to. The warring parties could live wonderfully in peace and prosperity if it were not for the psychology of their clashing worldviews and basic beliefs.

With this in mind, it is not surprising that individuals also react violently when their basic beliefs are questioned. Anyone who believes in justice, or in loyalty and reliability, or in mutual decency, will react harshly when these are questioned. If it is on top of that the case that an important area of life is affected and you also find yourself in a helpless situation, then there is embitterment.

Disparagement in the presence of colleagues, the infidelity of a spouse, the ingratitude of a boss, or the injustice of a former girlfriend can no longer be undone. In such situations, embitterment is a kind of emergency response. Although it is no longer possible to straighten out the bad event that has occurred, embitterment motivates one to try to catch up anyway. People try to fight back regardless of any losses that may be incurred to themselves. Their last resources are mobilized, such as in the pursuit of expensive legal disputes, which, if looked at it unemotionally, can be seen to have little chance of success. The psychoanalyst Karl Abraham called embitterment a masochistic reaction, an attempt to fight that involves the risk of self-destruction. And if nothing helps, then an attempt is made to achieve at least a tie with regard to levels of injustice. The goal is revenge. In family disputes, it can be observed again and again that the first priority should be to do everything in the best interests of the child. However, if there is a sense of mutual injustice and insult, that may lead to a fight to the finish, and the well-being of the child no longer plays a role.

Such feelings of embitterment are initially focused on the perpetrator, but then also on all of the other parties involved, and in the end, against the whole world. Those affected can no longer detach themselves from what has happened. They are trapped in the past and in embitterment. They are constantly tormented by memories of what happened. At some point, the moment is reached when it no longer matters what happened in the past. The 50 dollars (in the Case Example 1 described in Section 2.1: Injustice) become irrelevant. After a few weeks, the disparaging remark by the boss does no longer matter in reality. What remains and makes those affected deeply unhappy are memories and their own emotional state that is out of control. You suffer from yourself and can no longer distance yourself from it.

3
When Does an Embittered Person Need Professional Help?

You should tackle embitterment wherever it occurs, as it is not a pleasant feeling and usually does not lead to anything positive. In any case, you should actively take action against embitterment if it captures you. At that point, it is time to do something about it. Below are some indicators of when it is time to act to resolve your embitterment.

3.1   Duration, Generalization, and Intensity

Almost everyone has at some point been offended because of something. This feeling of insult can usually be overcome quickly, so that in the end, you may even laugh about it and learn from it.

It becomes difficult when you can no longer save yourself from embitterment. A persistent state of suffering arises. One is constantly reminded of the incident by something or anything. This, in turn, triggers feelings of dejection, despair, or anger, and a desire for justice. The embitterment can last for months and years. The feeling of embitterment can become so strong and intrusive that it affects many areas of life, such as work, leisure, and relationships with acquaintances and family. Help is then needed immediately.

3.2   Self-Harm

The desire for justice and the impulse to strike back can become so strong that one acts blindly against the aggressor without considering one's own losses; even one's own self-destruction is accepted. In one case, a man wanted to publicly expose and attack a prosecutor in a court case. When he was told that this might end up in a libel action being brought against him, if not a jail sentence, his answer was "I don't care." The desire to get justice is sometimes attempted in ways that may seem insane to outsiders. Hopeless legal disputes are started, and many thousands of dollars are wasted in the process, only for a negligibly small chance of getting what you would define as justice. In inheritance disputes, families fall apart over silver cutlery. Those affected may fantasize about how they can harm others, up to and including detailed murder plans – even though there is certainly no life event that would be worth spending many years in a prison for. In the mind of a clinically embittered person, however, obtaining "justice" in the form of vengeance, while accepting self-destruction often seems normal. So anyone who catches themself doing or planning things that not only harm the aggressor, but first and foremost themself, should seek help.

3.3 Not Liking Yourself

Embitterment can be seen as a combination of desperation and aggression. On the one hand, the reaction is directed outwards. The aggressor, other people, or the world are to blame for one's own suffering. "The others" did this to you. You are the victim of others.

On the other hand, there is regularly also self-blame. The phrase "would have" can be painful. If only I had behaved differently, if I had not trusted so blindly, I would have noticed something earlier – until I cannot stand myself anymore.

In addition, one is constantly tormented by bad moods and bad memories. Actually, you do not want to have anything to do with any of this anymore. You would prefer not to remember. You want to be carefree again, but you cannot. You also notice that your own behavior is not really effective. You experience aspects of yourself that you did not think were possible. Usually you are a peaceful person. Now everything you can see is aggression. One victim wrote: "I am really obsessed with my aggressive fantasies. I don't want to anymore. But I can't help it. I hate myself."

3.4 What Can Be Done?

It's bad enough when you have lost your job. However, it is not fair and a downright double punishment to be sleepless over it or to loose your friends. If something bad has happened to you, you do not deserve to feel bad all of the time afterwards. Something should be done about this.

Anyone who feels embittered has already taken an important step in the right direction by reading this booklet. They will have felt at least once that embitterment is not a good thing. That view can then be expanded. It is no longer just about dealing with the critical life event and the injustice suffered. No, it is also about freeing yourself from the embitterment trap.

A fundamentally important point is that, as already described above in Section 1.2.2: Withdrawing and Shutting Oneself Off, feelings of embitterment lead to those affected closing themselves in and isolating themselves from others. If other people approach them to help them, they may be rejected rather harshly. That does not make the situation any better. Nevertheless, a very important recommendation and in any case the first step toward a solution is to talk to others about what has happened. This includes describing what exactly happened, and it also means being able to perceive and accept your own feelings undisguised. This also includes thinking about how things can go on. All of this can be done more easily if someone listens to you.

> **Some Suggestions for Dealing With Feelings of Embitterment**
>
> - Maintain contact with people who are kind to you.
> - Describe what has happened objectively, without complaining, and in great detail to yourself and others.
> - Assess and name your feelings.
> - Specifically consider how things will work out if they go on as before.
> - Consider in detail how to proceed.
> - Draw up a cost–benefit analysis of your own behavior.
> - Look for other people to listen to you.
> - Take advice from other people seriously, even if you think it is wrong.
> - Do not get angry if you do not like someone's advice.
> - Do not expect any quick fixes.
> - Have some leniency and patience with yourself.
> - Write down what is actually going on inside you and then look at it again after a few days with a self-critical perspective.
> - Talk to others or yourself (out loud) until you get tired of the issue yourself.
> - Do something good for yourself, because someone who is in a bad mood deserves something good to compensate for that.
> - Do not let yourself down, because that may even give satisfaction to the perpetrator.
> - Remain realistic and do not expect the wrongdoer to regret something.
> - Activate your wisdom skills.

Talking to other people about your problem means that they can occasionally bring in additional points of view. Good advice cannot hurt. However, the experience of many affected people is that the good advice of others often misses the point. When your partner has offended and abandoned you, it is easy for someone to recommend that you find a new partner. This does not make the pain and the injustice go away. But it is also not totally wrong.

As a victim, you should not expect conversations with other people to present quick solutions. You have to realize that others cannot always understand the scope of the problem at hand, and that some advice will completely ignore the topic. Nevertheless, it is worth talking to others about your own experience. That forces you to explain to yourself what happened and what is wrong with you – which is what actually helps. You are forced to put your thoughts in order, and you are encouraged to look at yourself from an outside perspective. The following sentence is a good summary of this: "Once I have explained what is going on to someone else, I will have finally understood it myself."

Talking to other people about what has happened also has the effect that repeating the same stories over and over again can, at some point, become downright boring. The more often and the longer you talk about something that has happened, the more the emotions will cool down. Repeatedly talking about an issue has therapeutic effects in and of itself.

One method of cooling off emotions can also be to write down what happened. That also forces you to actively think of the problem. Writing down takes time, you have to think about it, correct wrong information, and bring coherence to the story. Afterwards, you can give such a report to others to read. Sometimes they may even understand what is bothering you better than if you just gushed it out emotionally. Many people deal with bad experiences by writing them down. This is something psychotherapists use again and again.

People with embitterment disorder rightly seek the solution not from within themselves at first, but from other people and external circumstances. But some realism is also important. There is no point in expecting the wrongdoer to change, apologize, take something back, or be ashamed. Waiting for others to take action, or even for the aggressor to apologize, does not seem sensible. You might wait a long time or, in most cases, forever.

It also does not help to "bathe" in your resentment based on the idea that that will "let them see what they have done!" That will rarely work, and it will only make you feel bad. Another misunderstanding is that it would be seen as a confession that the whole thing was not that bad after all, if you bring the past event to a close. But at the same time, it is also true that ultimately you will give the aggressor the opportunity to harm you twice through your own suffering. If you have lost your job or partner as a result of a situation, for example, then you will be punished twice if you then have to endure sleep disorders, problems with friends, or significant loss of money. Such a power should not be given to the aggressor.

It also makes no sense to remain wrapped up in your suffering. The only one who really suffers in those cases is yourself, while everyone else can continue to be optimistic about the future. Your own suffering does not score any points. You do not have to suffer to show the world what it has done to you. In the end, nobody cares anyway. It is certainly not worth it to throw away your own happiness after you have already suffered. The cost of the injustice suffered is likely to be high enough.

It is also not worth waiting for miracles; they are rare. It is true that one can certainly not expect "evildoers" to suddenly become nice people. The dead do not rise up again, and partners who run away do not come back. And would you really want to have them back again?

After all, a little self-care is not wrong either. Those who are badly off deserve something good in compensation and justice. If no one else does it, then you do it yourself. Shoes that you buy yourself can also be beautiful. Instead of investing money in legal battles because of a 4-inch incorrectly set garden fence, one could buy a garden swing.

To improve such situations, you should do your part and control the future and your happiness yourself. In the end, everyone is the architect of their own fortune and is responsible for themselves and what they do. You should not let your embitterment guide you, because it leads to self-destruction, as already explained above.

All of these recommendations sound so obvious and trivial. Yet they are often difficult to implement. It could be that this sort of advice is also experienced as a "punch in the face" and increases your sense of hopelessness because you know what would be right and still cannot do it. It is often like that in life. Just think of the resolutions we make regarding exercise, healthy eating, hobbies, etc. If we did everything we think was right, we would be fine.

Embitterment is resistance that prevents us from doing what would be useful. It is like a virus that paralyzes the immune system. Therefore, further approaches are sometimes required.

Instead of an embittered reaction, one should try for a clever reaction instead. This includes reflecting on the wisdom competencies that everyone has to solve difficult problems. When you are stuck with a problem, wisdom is needed more than ever. Cleverness in this sense means the consistent application of all available wisdom skills.

4
Wisdom

4.1 Wisdom as a Problem-Solving Capacity

Wisdom is a skill that is common to every human being, albeit to varying degrees. It is needed to deal with difficult problems. In short, wisdom is the ability to solve seemingly unsolvable problems. Wisdom helps to find the best possible solution in difficult life situations, to enable us to make good judgments on important life issues, and to find appropriate coping strategies for insoluble problems. In these ways, wisdom helps to deal with stress and conflicts.

Every day, each of us encounters a wide variety of unsolvable problems. For example, whether you should stay at home with your sick child or go to work is an unsolvable problem. Should you buy the expensive bio orange juice or the inexpensive cheap juice? Are there really any relevant differences in the contents of the juice cartons, or do you only pay for the brand name? Is money or the environment more important to you, or do you want to impress guests or not? In the end, there is no definite solution. This is even more true when it comes to important life issues. Should you stay single or not, marry this or that person, should you have children, take a certain job, or change your place of residence? Here, too, there are no guarantees and no simple answers, although your future life depends on such decisions. How do you deal with irreversible problems? The death of a person, the infidelity of a partner, and a dismissal cannot be changed. Even if the partner comes back, the fact of the infidelity persists.

All of these small and large dilemmas require wisdom to find optimal solutions and what is right for yourself and for others. Wisdom is thus a problem-solving ability that is put to use every day.

Psychological research has shown that there is a link between life satisfaction and wisdom. Wisdom has a greater impact on well-being than health, socioeconomic status, financial situation, environment, or level of social engagement. Wisdom protects against the negative consequences of life stress. Wise people are better able to get rid of negative experiences from the past. Wisdom is the opposite of being rigid, stubborn, and selfish. Wisdom also makes it possible to get along better with other people and to find mutually acceptable compromises in the event of a conflict.

4.2 Wisdom in Addressing Embitterment

Since embittered people are trapped in difficult life problems, it makes sense to fall back on wisdom competencies when looking for solutions and a way out.

At the beginning, it needs to be clarified what exactly the triggering event was about. What was the real cause that made you react the way you did? The fact that something bad happened or you were attacked does not in itself explain what led to such long-lasting embitterment. Therefore, it must first be clarified honestly what happened, when, where, and how. What exactly "made you unstable" or "broke your heart"? The fact that your partner has left does not yet explain what the real problem is and what one is really experiencing as unfair. Is it that the breakup came without warning, that you were not asked, that your money is gone, that you have been accused of something, that your neighbors are talking about you? There may be some answers to this that you will not like.

Afterwards, an inventory of the problems associated with the embitterment must be made. This includes the recurring memories, the suffering from those memories, the type of agonizing emotions, the withdrawal from the family, friends, and work, and the costs of the ongoing dispute. A clear statement of costs is required. This can be painful and trigger new negative feelings, such as shame, but it is still advisable.

Many embittered people have fantasies of revenge and aggression. This is perfectly normal. Depending on the case, the intensity of these can range from simple fantasies of aggression, to ideas of murder. You may be embittered, but you are still not a murderer, and you do not want to do stupid things either. If you admit to yourself what dark fantasies you have in your heart and openly admit those, then that can take the pressure off you. You can think and dream, even of very bad things. You certainly can enjoy those thoughts for a bit. That does not mean that you do what they suggest.

Finally, the question still remains of how to get out of the whole mess. Wisdom can help. Wisdom is discussed and described in religions or philosophy. In this book, we are talking about the results of psychological wisdom research. Researchers have defined a dozen dimensions of wisdom (see Table 1). They refer to a differentiated perspective on the world, other people, yourself, your own experience, and the future. The following table gives an overview of the most important wisdom competencies.

Each of these dimensions of wisdom describes a subaspect of wisdom and special points of view. The following is intended to explain in more detail what is to be understood by this in detail, and how each dimension can play its part in clarifying and overcoming a problem. This description is written in such a way that it can also serve as a suggestion for the reader to have their own thoughts, in the sense of self-help guidance.

Table 1. Dimensions of Wisdom

View of the world

1. Knowledge of facts and procedures.
   General and specific knowledge of problems and problem constellations, what those problems consist of, and what possibilities there are for solving them.
2. Contextualization.
   Knowledge of the temporal and situational context of problems and the numerous circumstances in which we find ourselves involved.
3. Value relativism.
   Knowledge of the diversity of values and goals in life and the need to consider each person within their value system, without losing sight of one's own values.

View of other people

4. Change of perspective.
   Ability to describe a problem from the perspective of the different people involved.
5. Emotional empathy.
   Ability to empathize with another person's emotional experience.

View of yourself

6. Self-distance.
   Ability to recognize and understand the perceptions and evaluations of oneself from the perspective of other people.
7. Self-relativization.
   Ability to accept that you are not always the most important person and that a lot of things do not go according to your own will, nor are they based on your own interests.
8. Relativization of problems and aspirations.
   Ability to be humble and to accept that one's own problems should not be taken so seriously in comparison with many other problems in the world.

View of your own experience

9. Emotional awareness and acceptance of emotions.
   Ability to perceive and accept one's own feelings.
10. Emotional serenity and humor.
    Ability to achieve emotional balance, not to get carried away by emotions, to control one's own emotions according to the requirements of the situation, as well as the ability to look on oneself and one's own difficulties with humor.

View of the future

11. Long-term perspective.
    Knowledge of negative and positive aspects of every event and behavior, the distinction between short- and long-term consequences, and the many contradictory consequences.
12. Bringing the past to a close and being able to forgive.
    Ability to let things rest, to accept what has happened as it is, and to free yourself from the pressure of always having to fight back.
13. Uncertainty tolerance.
    Knowledge of the uncertainty in life about the past, present, and future.

4.3 Wisdom Skills in Problem Solving

To illustrate how to approach problems using wisdom, two case descriptions are presented first. They are based on real cases. For each wisdom competence, it is then shown how it can be used to cope with things that are completely unacceptable and cannot be reversed.

Case Example 5: Infidelity

There are stories that you think only appear in Hollywood movies. Ms. U. wanted to get married. Everything was prepared. There was a big celebration coming up. Family, friends, acquaintances, and neighbors had been invited. Loads of money was spent. On the evening before the wedding, Ms. U. caught her future husband in bed with her best friend and maid of honor.

What followed was tragic. The wedding was canceled. All hopes and wishes for their common future relationship dissolved into nothing. Ms. U. was deeply offended by this incredible breach of trust. Not only because of the groom but also the friend. The financial expenses had to be written off. Everyone talked about Ms. U., in her circle of friends and also in the neighborhood. She could not go anywhere. She bitterly withdrew herself. She also broke off relationships with other friends and acquaintances. She definitely did not want to come in contact with other men anymore. She lived in isolation for the years that followed. Intrusive memories of her shame, humiliation, and the breach of trust constantly remind her of those past events. Even years later, Ms. U. still bitterly cannot forget what happened. She is in pain when she sees other couples. At night, she dreams of stabbing her prospective husband with a kitchen knife. Even after several years, she is still brooding over what to do to publicly expose him or how to seek revenge. In the end, she is in such a desolate state that she is referred to a psychosomatic hospital.

Case Example 6: President of a Club

Mr. V. is the founder of a club. He has invested a lot of time, manpower, money, and passion in its development. Mr. V. is the president, his deputy is a good friend of his. Both manage to make the club flourish. This also means that new members join.

The board of directors is to be re-elected at a general assembly. Without Mr. V. having suspected anything of this, his friend runs for office as president and is elected by majority vote. It becomes clear that his alleged friend and cochair has been working behind his back on this election for a long time. Mr. V. experiences this as a devious action and a breach of trust. He experiences it as a great injustice that he is simply dumped after he has founded and built the club and has done so much for "his" club. Mr. V. is deeply disappointed, offended, and embittered. He declares his resignation from the club right away. A costly legal process, which he loses, follows because he refuses to give up the club's documents. Since the club was also essentially his social circle, he is suddenly without friends and acquaintances. He does nothing to look for new contacts. His bad mood does not subside at home either, which leads to significant family problems. He "bathes" in fantasies that he could set fire to the clubhouse. Because of his insufferability and displeasure, problems also arise in the workplace. He takes sick leave and is eventually forced by his health insurance to undergo inpatient psychosomatic rehabilitation treatment.

In the following sections, these two real-life cases will be examined in more detail from the perspective of wisdom skills. The reader is invited to think along. A quickly accessible overview for each problem example/dimension is presented in the table above.

4.4 Knowledge of Facts and Procedures – What Is Actually Going on?

When you are struggling with a life problem, the first thing to do is to understand what has happened and how it actually happened. After all, how are you supposed to solve problems if you have not fully figured out what was going on? It is important to recognize that many factors will generally have an influence and interact when a problem arises.

It is therefore wise to first take a step back and clearly think about what happened and describe what the situation is like. This sounds easy, but it is extremely difficult when one is embittered and trapped in one's emotions. Especially when you are emotionally hurt, you will not want to notice certain things, because the memory of them hurts. Fact and problem-solving knowledge is about clarifying how the problem was triggered in the first place and who was involved. The question is, for example, what exactly happened? Who were the participants? When, at what minute and in what situation, did it break your heart? What exactly is it what hurts you so much now? Are there any witnesses of the event? How would the situation appear from the point of view of uninvolved viewers? What was the build-up to the whole thing? When did problems start to emerge, and how have they developed? What are the general legal, structural, material, and personal conditions involved? What was the reaction of others who were involved? Are the current problems related to the original critical event or rather to the subsequent actions of those involved? Who is now still involved, who may not have been involved at the beginning? How does the critical life event affect your life? Which areas of life does the offending event influence? There will be still many other similar questions that need to be answered at the start.

Fact and problem-solving knowledge also includes rationally considering the options for action. There is no perfect solution that can be achieved by one particular approach. To solve difficult life situations, there will be many factors and many steps to be considered. How can one deal with the problem as effectively as possible? Can something be achieved through legal means? Are there other people who can help you, and if so, how and by doing what? Can you make direct contact with the person who caused the problem? What aggressive or friendly options are there? What exactly do you want to achieve: money, an apology, the undoing of the event, or something else? What are the costs of each strategy, and how good are the chances of success? What can you do directly for your own well-being? Here, too, there are many different aspects, with various answers.

Case Example 5 Follow-Up: Infidelity

First of all, it makes sense or is even necessary to make sure of all of the facts. How long have you (Ms. U. and prospective husband) known each other? Have you already lived together and possibly had sexual contacts and perhaps for a long time? How long have your friend and now ex-boyfriend known each other? How long have you known your friend? Why do you call your friend a friend? How have family or friends and acquaintances actually reacted? Who supports you? How can you spread your point of view among friends?

Further, there are also very mundane questions. How much money did the wedding preparation cost, and who might be left with the costs? Do you have a shared apartment, and where can you go if you have to move out? What is the worst aspect out of everything: the behavior of the ex-boyfriend, that of the friend, the public exposure, the money, or what else? Are all men unfaithful? What can you do differently with another man? As you can see, the description of the situation is not done in one sentence. You have to pay attention to many points.

Case Example 6 Follow-Up: Club

First of all, it is necessary to take a look at the club rules. How is the chairman elected, for what duration, and with what quorum? Was the election correctly held? Have the new members been accepted into the club correctly? What makes the new chairman more attractive to the other members? What rights and obligations do you have as a former chairman? What new roles will there be in the club in the future? Do you know which members elected the new chairman, and who voted for you? Who are the club members you might be able to continue working with? Is there perhaps the possibility of a rerun for election in the future? What can you do to support the new board and the club, since the club itself is important to you? Are there similar clubs, which you can join and in which you could continue your hobby? Here, too, there are many questions that should be asked and answered in as much detail as possible – if necessary, with the support of someone else.

Tipp

If you want to solve a difficult problem, it is wise to look at the given facts first.

4.5 Contextualization – Which Circumstances Play a Role Here?

A factual description will show that any critical life event is inserted into a broader range of concrete circumstances. If you are struggling with a life problem, then it is important to clarify which conditions led to the events and why you are evaluating and experiencing the situation as you are. How might the critical event be evaluated under different conditions? Answering this question helps to identify the real or essential point of a problem and to separate it from secondary aspects. *Contextualization* means that the evaluation of many things depends on the environment – that is, the context. The fact that certain situations unfold just as they do depends on many framework conditions. The process and evaluation of the situation depends on the context of the situation.

If someone is asked if they speak French, then the admission that they can at best speak this language poorly can be of very different importance, depending on whether the question is raised in a job interview or by friends. The assessment of skills and behavior in a job interview can be further very different, depending on whether you are seeking to be merely an employee or a manager, whether the company is economically in good shape or is threatened with bankruptcy, and even whether the human resources manager is in a bad mood because of problems with recruitment or problems at home.

> **Case Example 5 Follow-Up: Infidelity**
>
> It is important to assess under what circumstances the act of infidelity took place. Were those involved intoxicated? If they were not, it is still interesting to consider how you would have reacted if the two had actually been drunk. Would it have hurt you just as much? How would the whole thing be judged if you had already had a lot of intimate contacts yourself with your now ex-boyfriend or if you had been to a swinger club with your partner? What if the wedding was planned in Las Vegas without anyone's family present? What is the aspect that was really unacceptable, the sexual contact, the violation of moral rules, the surprise, the family reaction, or what?

> **Case Example 6 Follow-Up: Club**
>
> The meaning of the deselection depends, of course, on the context. Is that the only important position in your (Mr. V.'s) life? Would you react in the same way if you were also on the board of other clubs at the same time, or if you had been elected deputy chairman? What if you imagined that you did not have any friends outside the club, or that you had a large social network? What did your family or friends think of your club activity? What if the partner would be happy that all of this was finally over, or the partner was also active in a club?

> **Tipp**
>
> If you want to solve a difficult problem, it is wise to first look at the framework and context.

4.6 Value Relativism – What Is It All About?

If the specific circumstances that determine the significance of what has happened have become clear to you, then of course there is also the view that the incident might have to be weighted differently under different value perspectives, and that the same event can have different meanings depending on different worldviews and beliefs. Value relativism means being able to accept that the same situation can be judged differently from other worldviews. There can be different points of view and values from yourself, without it being necessary to say who is "correct." People in different cultures or situations have different values. Does a woman have to be veiled, or can she, in some public settings, show herself naked? Are you allowed to drive a large car, or is only going by train correct? Everyone has their own opinion, and they would not put up with it, if others tried to force them to give up theirs and take up another's worldview. When during political debates on television, different political opinions, values, and worldviews collide "bitterly" and otherwise well-behaved people get loud and aggressive and misbehave, then this is the opposite of value relativism.

Value relativism does not mean giving up one's own worldview and values, or even accepting another, or questioning values in general. It is about accepting that there are different values, acknowledging them, being able to deal with them, and not taking it as a personal attack if someone does not share your worldview. It also does not mean to change your own position. This value relativism is very difficult, and it is more natural to start a conflict or even a war, in such cases, than to deal peacefully with one another. Similar to value relativism is the attitude of someone who is proud to speak German but still thinks English or French are wonderful languages.

> **Case Example 5 Follow-Up: Infidelity**
>
> For Ms. U., loyalty and monogamy are clearly of a great value. There are many people who experience this the same way, and there are also cultures in which it is an important moral rule. However, there are also people who experience monogamy as a restriction and cultures in which it is natural to have many sexual partners. Different values can even be found within the same country. The moral rules that apply in a disco might be viewed very critically in a church.
>
> Which morals are correct? All are correct. One could assume that the fiancé has different moral and relationship ideas than Ms. U. Both have their worldviews. Seen from the outside, one cannot say that one worldview is better or more correct than the other.
>
> That does not mean, however, that you have to put your own values aside. Simply, that it is helpful to be aware of your partner's values when entering into a relationship. To believe that they can be changed is an illusion.

> **Case Example 6 Follow-Up: Club**
>
> Also in club life, everyone has their own values. They may or may not be shared by others in the same club. In other clubs, these might be very different anyway. For example, the essence of a club can be defined by fellowship, where you have to be able to rely on members of the club. With some clubs this is true for a lifetime. Loyalty, reliability, and transparency among club members are therefore very important, and insidious behavior and intrigue are com-

pletely unimaginable. Other clubs are more like interest groups in which everyone tries to find their own advantage. Konrad Adenauer, the former German chancellor, once said that enemies are not as bad as fellow party members.

That means the position of chairman, the survival of the club, or a particular club value are all important and legitimate goals. This can, of course, lead to conflicts. Can I accept that I want the club to pursue social goals – for example, caring for those in need – while my competitor sees the club as a profit-oriented business enterprise?

Tipp

When trying to solve a difficult problem, it is wise to first think what is important to whom and who holds which values.

4.7 Change of Perspective – What Do Others Actually Think?

The subject of value relativism already suggests that different people have different views of the world. This is even more so when it comes to specific situations and individuals. If you are asked why you acted the way you did in a certain situation, you will usually be able to give good reasons. But this also applies to other people who act differently from what you would do yourself. That means, if someone has behaved in such a way that you cannot understand it at all, then it would certainly not be wrong to clarify what the other person or your opponent thinks.

As natural as it seems, it is difficult to do this. People want others to think and feel the way they do themselves. That means you project your own thoughts and experiences onto others. But that, as you might guess, does not have to be correct.

A change of perspective means to slip into the role of another person and try to see the world through their eyes. Changing perspective means, for example, putting yourself in the roll of the boss, wife, or friend. This can definitely also be extended to being the person who is seen as the trigger for the embitterment. Without question, when this happens, it is a special but also a healing achievement.

It is all about understanding what made the other person do what they did and about understanding any good reasons for doing it. For example, a dismissal does not have to have anything to do with you personally; it might be for completely independent, personnel-related reasons.

An additional form of changing perspective can also consist of looking at the current problem from a different perspective. How would another person see the problem in my place: for example, a pastor, a lawyer, my grandmother, my Turkish friend, or my neighbor?

Such a change of perspective is often difficult for people, because they are subject to the misunderstanding that one is agreeing to something if one can understand it. This is not the case. Rather, it is important to realize that if you "understand" something, you do not automatically agree with it. If an examiner can comprehend and understand what an examinee is thinking, then he can still give him a bad grade – if not because of having that understanding. If a judge understands what happened to a defendant in a criminal act, that will increase the correctness of the judgment, even if it means a life sentence.

> **Case Example 5 Follow-Up: Infidelity**
>
> In the case of infidelity, Ms. U. might think that her partner sees her friend as more attractive than her or that the friend is taking revenge because they had a problem with each other years ago. All of this may or may not be true. It can just as well be that the ex-boyfriend and friend have not given any thought for her, that they have always been in love with each other and have now discovered their true love just before the impending wedding. Both had this last chance, in the sense of something like a bachelor party, to have sex together, etc. There are many ways of thinking about this. A change of perspective can help to better understand the processes, which in turn can help with problem solving.

> **Case Example 6 Follow-Up: Club**
>
> The friend who is now the club's chairman must have had very good reasons to boot his friend out. You do not do something like that without a good reason. But what are the good reasons? Here, too, one can imagine a lot of things that might have caused the friend to behave the way he did, and what he might have been thinking. There are no limits to the imagination. However, even better would be an attempt at clarification.
>
> Such a change of perspective should also include the other club members. And it should not only concern the past, but also the present and future. Now that the friend is in office, what kind of ideas does he have for how things will continue? Does he want to restructure the club, how does he want to deal with his predecessor, and what do the other club members expect?

> **Tipp**
>
> If you want to solve a difficult problem, it is wise to first put yourself in the position of others and especially that of your opponent.

4.8 Emotional Empathy – How Do Others Actually Feel?

"Empathy" is an expression that is commonly used. Many people understand empathic people to be those who are there for others in difficult situations, who offer help, or approach other people warmheartedly.

Emotional empathy is closely related to a change of perspective. A change of perspective is about the other's view of the world, while emotional empathy is about the other's feelings. An examiner can put themselves in the shoes of the examinee and understand what they think, what the content of an answer is, and whether they are knowledgeable or not. Regardless of this, though, they may also perceive whether the examinee is afraid, self-confident, or arrogant. It is about the ability to identify with the feelings of others. This means it is something other than understanding their motives. The other person is also a person and therefore has feelings that significantly shape their actions and their assessments of the world. It is wise to be clear about this.

Empathy is about understanding what the aggressor felt before, during, or after the incident, and what emotionally drove the person to act the way they did. Was the person stressed, under pressure, sad, or otherwise emotionally involved? How could that have influenced their behavior? Would the person have reacted differently in a different mood? What feelings emerged after the critical event?

One problem is that many people have difficulty correctly perceiving other people's feelings, because they project their own feelings into the other. If the other has done something that I think is bad, then "he should be ashamed." But is he? Or is he happy?

> **Case Example 5 Follow-Up: Infidelity**
>
> Ms. U. would possibly be ashamed of herself if she had been unfaithful, which is why she might believe that her partner and girlfriend would or should be ashamed as well. But what feelings did the ex-fiancé and girlfriend actually have? Were they in love, or was it just about sexual desires? Did they feel guilty, anxious about the possibility of being caught, or were they just on cloud nine?

> The same applies to the time after the incident and today. Are they ashamed or happy and satisfied? You cannot be sure, or even expect, that both of them will be ashamed. Perhaps both the ex-fiancé and the friend are happy that the incident happened. Maybe the ex-fiancé is even happy that he is now free, not married, and has found his soulmate.

> **Case Example 6 Follow-Up: Club**
>
> Here, too, Mr. V. could think that his former friend must feel guilty and feel bad. Is that correct, though? How did the former best friend feel when he got the majority of the votes? What were his feelings when he thought of you? Is he ashamed or embarrassed that he had taken the office as chairman from you, or is he proud, satisfied, and happy? The club members do not have to be ashamed or have a guilty conscience either. Why would they? After all, they just voted. They may or may not be embarrassed about the result. Mr. V. cannot expect others to feel the way he feels or how he would like them to feel.

> **Tipp**
>
> When trying to solve a difficult problem, it is wise to first be clear about the feelings of others.

4.9 Self-Distance – How Do Others See Me?

Self-distance also has something to do with a change of perspective. It is about looking at yourself and your own behavior from the outside. Even just by looking at photos, looking in the mirror, or observing oneself in a video recording, many people think that this person somehow looks different from what we imagine themselves to be.

How one would like to appear to others, how I think that I appear to others, and how I actually appear to others are not the same thing. How you behave also affects how other people perceive you differently. Someone may see you as happy and self-confident. Someone else might say you seem egotistic and arrogant, while you see yourself as friendly and understanding. Distancing yourself from yourself and seeing yourself through the eyes of others can help you better spot problems and understand how those affect other people.

> **Case Example 5 Follow-Up: Infidelity**
>
> Ms. U. likes to see herself as a loving partner. What does she look like, though, in the eyes of the ex-fiancé or the friend? Perhaps she might be perceived as possessive and restrictive. For Ms. U., her desperate reaction was natural. Uninvolved viewers, on the other hand, might see her as hysterical or cold. She can think of herself as ugly or beautiful, while nobody else notices or sees her that way. Of course, it is also allowed to ask what kind of impression you would like to make on others, and whether your appearance corresponds to that or not.

> **Case Example 6 Follow-Up: Club**
>
> Mr. V. may have considered himself a very good chairman and indispensable. Who else is of the same opinion? He may experience himself as communicative, while others see him as domineering. He thinks he has an overview of everything; others see relevant gaps in his skills. However, he may also worry that he has not taken enough care of the interests of the club members, while they do not see it that way and have never had a problem with that.
>
> It is also of interest to ask how he affected others when he found out that he no longer was the chairman of the club. Do the others understand why he stormed out of the meeting, or did that just reinforce everyone's belief that a change was urgently needed? Such a realistic look from the outside can point out effective ways in further problem solving under given circumstances.

> **Tipp**
>
> When trying to solve a difficult problem, it is wise to look at yourself through the eyes of others first.

4.10 Self-Relativization – How Important Am I?

Self-distancing already includes perceiving yourself realistically. This also includes the question of how important you are in the world, and what your place is. It is wise to understand and accept that, while you are important as a person, you are only a small part of a complex world. The world does not revolve around you. In most areas of life, if you look closely, you are not the decisive factor. When a company is relocated, the workplace is restructured, laws are passed, friends meet, all this can affect you as an individual. Nevertheless, the decisions made do not depend on you and do not have to take you into consideration. With many processes, it is usually not even possible to respond to everyone's wishes, since these can differ from one to the other and even contradict each other. Many things happen without looking at the individual person and their needs. There are more important things in the world than your own fate. Nobody can be forced to adapt their behavior to the needs of another person. Nobody "has" to be nice or supportive, considerate, or help out with money. It is nice, of course, when people do do that. But what they do depends on how important you are to them. An individual employee will never have a say in how the company will proceed, because he is not important enough. Someone who has a larger stake in the company, on the other hand, will be heard because they are important.

It helps with problem solving if you see your own role in the world realistically, if you categorize yourself correctly, and that you can accept that you cannot impose your will on the world, and sometimes you have to stand back.

Case Example 5 Follow-Up: Infidelity

People who are getting married are or should be the most important person in the world to each other at that moment. However, there are other things that are important in this situation as well. In addition to the partner, parents are also important, money is important, your job is important, your religion or beliefs are important, and your friends. In many cultures, parents, money, and religion are more important than the togetherness of the couple when getting married. The individual has to subordinate themselves. That means Ms. U. has to examine how important she is in this world, for her ex-fiancé, her parents, her friends. Who even takes notice of what happened? To whom is she so important that she can count on their support? Are you so significant that you can force your partner or friend to be loyal eternally? Do you have so many resources and so much influence that you can punish both?

Case Example 6 Follow-Up: Club

Before being replaced, Mr. V. was an important person for the club. Now someone else is the chairman. Why not? Was he so important that only he could do that job? Could someone else do the job as well or even better? Why should he alone have the chance to be chairman? Is not it wise in such situations to question your own importance as a boss? You yourself have ideas about how indispensable you are. Does this mean that every voter has to think that way? Cannot it also be that the competitor is better than you in some things? In the case of the club situation, you have to realize that you are one of many. Every member of the club has the right to be club chairman. Even if you are the founder of the club, according to the statutes you are just one member of the club. What are the consequences?

> **Tipp**
>
> If you want to solve a difficult problem, it is wise to first question your own importance and role.

4.11 Relativization of Problems and Aspirations – What Am I Actually Entitled to?

With self-relativization, the question arises of what claims one might have and what one is entitled to. We all have expectations and aspirations. If these are not met, we may react emotionally, often with anger. Frustration is defined as "hindrance in achieving a goal." That means if you think you have to have something, and things turn out differently, then that is painful. One way to make yourself miserable is to set your standards so high that you definitely will not achieve them. On the other hand, goals and aspirations are an important driving force for moving forward, for change, and for developing things. Those who do not want a good education for themselves or their children run the risk of being unsuccessful in the end. Demands have two faces. Things do not work without aspirations, but you should not overdo it. Additionally, there are aspirations and needs in regard to important things and those that can easily be ignored. That would mean, you have to clarify among the following: Which demands do I have? What am I entitled to? Which are important so that I would fight for them? Which ones are trifles that would not make the hassle worthwhile?

An approach to checking entitlements and, if necessary their relativization, is comparison with other people. What would other people say if they had my salary, my apartment, my car? Would they all be dissatisfied, or would one or the other consider themselves lucky?

Gratitude is also helpful when reviewing entitlements. This means not only looking at the deficits but also the positives. If you fall down the stairs and break your foot, you may be grateful that you have not broken your neck. Reconciliation with your own demands on life can begin with thinking that you are grateful that you did not have an accident today, that you had no conflict with another person, and that everything went well and you felt very relaxed.

It can undoubtedly be disappointing and exhausting to go through a divorce after 7 years of marriage. However, you do not have to see the entire marriage as a total disaster afterwards. You can also be grateful that you were able to experience not only bad but also good times, that your child was born, etc. To be grateful means to compare oneself with other groups.

Living in a developed country, in itself has many advantages. To be grateful for this helps you to understand, to question your own claims, and to put them into perspective.

> **Case Example 5 Follow-Up: Infidelity**
>
> The wish that your partnership and then the marriage is and lasts as happily as possible until the end of your life is one that hopefully many people have when they get married. This claim also helps to invest something in a good marriage. Ultimately, however, it is more of a wish or goal, than a claim to which one would have any right. Almost every second marriage breaks up. Can I be surprised if it is not any different for me? Where did I get the claim that fate should not allow me to be cheated on? I should be grateful if it does not happen. In the case of Ms. U., she can even be grateful that the infidelity was discovered before the marriage. After that it would have been a lot more complicated.

> **Case Example 6 Follow-Up: Club**
>
> Mr. V. obviously had the idea that he is entitled to be elected over and over again. If you put it this way, you can immediately see that this was a very exaggerated and indeed downright absurd claim. Anyone who is elected has to run again after the end of their term of office, because these are the rules. Mr. V. is obviously suffering from his completely excessive demands. Even as a long-time chairman, a little more modesty would not be a bad thing.

> **Tipp**
>
> If you want to solve a difficult problem, it is wise to first question your own aspirations.

4.12 Emotional Awareness and Acceptance of Emotions – What Is Going on in My Heart?

It is human to be angry when something goes wrong, to grieve when a partner leaves you, or to feel joy when you receive a gift. There are several hundred different emotional blends and feelings, which even can be contradictory in themselves. When you think about your work, you may be happy because of the good earnings and your reputation, but you may also be annoyed by customers, you may be frustrated because things are not developing as expected, you may be proud of your successes, and so on. All of that at the same time. In the same way, you love your partner, worry about them, and get annoyed by their mess. There is always a potpourri of feelings. If you love your partner and at the same time would love them to be out of the way, psychologists refer to that as an approach–avoidance conflict. If you then imagine that you might leave your partner because they are not perfect, this also has both good and bad sides. At that point, you are caught in a double approach–avoidance conflict. This is pure stress. In animal experiments, pigeons lose their feathers under such circumstances.

A first step out of this is to be aware of your own emotions. This means that you look at all of your feelings, both positive and negative. They are there, even if you do not want them or even if they are not "politically correct." Some people believe that admitting that your partner is really getting on your nerves will put your relationship in danger. The opposite is the case. It is positive to accept that your partner is no more perfect than you are or than anyone else; indeed it would be downright unbearable to be with a perfect partner. This can even strengthen a relationship. Everything has its price. I can be happy about how caring my partner is and treat that like a gift. However, I will also need to tolerate their untidiness.

You have to accept your own feelings, as they cannot be turned off. This includes accepting that you have feelings of aggression and you want perhaps to imagine pushing your ex-partner, boss, or neighbor down the stairs. To accept that you have such ideas and emotions and to allow them, is healthy and does not mean that you will put your thoughts into practice.

> **Case Example 5 Follow-Up: Infidelity**
>
> Being cheated on is often associated with a variety of negative emotions. There is the experience of loss, but also disappointment, surprise, shame, feeling hurt, anger, aggression, feelings of desire for revenge, etc. This is normal and cannot be switched off. It is human. Of course, it is understandable if Ms. U. would like to grab a knife immediately after the incident and stab the tires of the cars of those who cheated on her, or poison them. But that does not mean putting it into practice. Admitting to such feelings even protects against rash actions.
>
> Once you have visualized your feelings, it is often not easy to tell what is particularly bad. Is it really the loss of the partner or is it more the social exposure or even the anger about the lost money? If Ms. U. takes a calm look at the spectrum of her own feelings, that alone makes it clearer what really hurt her, which of course leads to different reactions.

> **Case Example 6 Follow-Up: Club**
>
> Diverse emotions can also arise in Mr. V. case. These may include disappointment that he was not reelected, the pain of separating from the role of club chairman, anger about the ingratitude of the other members, shame because of the degradation, disappointment because of his former friend's actions, a sense of helplessness because he did not manage to get reelected, and a desire for revenge against his competitor, connected with fantasies of public humiliation. Realizing that you are angry because you have not achieved a goal and accepting it as human can help you to calm down and to realize what that anger is actually about.

> **Tipp**
>
> If you want to solve a difficult problem, it is wise to become clear about your own feelings, how they may contradict each other, and what unpleasant feelings you may also be experiencing.

4.13 Emotional Serenity and Humor – How Do I Keep Cool?

As already mentioned in the previous section, feelings are very powerful and drive one to the most varied and sometimes strangest actions. I get mad at my partner, give in to the emotion, and beat them. That is understandable from one point of view, but at the same time, it is not. Emotions are one thing, actions are another. I can find someone very attractive. Do I have to have sex with them right away? Probably not. You can also enjoy the sexual attractiveness without having to act. As an old saying puts it: "You get your appetite outside, but you eat at home."

This means that you can and must have your feelings under control. Emotional serenity can also be described as emotional self-control and composure. Keeping cool in difficult situations and not letting your feelings take control is an important wisdom skill. If you think of people you would consider wise, they are always people who have their emotions under control and who exude emotional balance. It makes more sense to show calm when dealing with problems, instead of engaging in a loud argument with your boss or partner, screaming and crying. As already said, the point is not to suppress your feelings, but to accept them and then to control and master them.

In order to not let your emotions run free, it usually helps to let a little time pass before you act. You get an email, and you get angry. You write an answer immediately, but save it first. The next morning you will never send the text that you wrote yesterday using the exact same words. A popular saying goes "sleep on it for the night."

Another type of emotional control is the induction of alternative emotions. Every student knows the method of simply imagining a bad examiner in his underpants.

Internal dialogues can also help. You can tell yourself and persuade yourself: "Don't get so upset!" This can help. You can also direct your attention to something more important or enjoyable. When your boss is being annoying, you can think of your quiet office or the end of the day.

Lastly, humor can also be used for managing emotions. "You've got to laugh otherwise you'd cry," as the saying goes. It is an emotion whose real purpose is to weaken painful or angry emotions. Television programs such as "Candid Camera" or "Punk'd" are good examples. Very annoying things happen to people and even make them desperate. Their reactions can be very different. There are those who are in absolute despair, and those that lose their composure. These are the people you would laugh at. Then there are the people with a sense of humor. The soup ended up on your pants? Even such a mishap has its funny side, and there are people who take it calmly and some even have to laugh. These are the people you admire and who come across as good. So, when you are in a bad mood, thinking of such a show might help. "Show your enemy your teeth and smile!"

Incidentally, all of the wisdom skills discussed so far also help against excessive emotions. Anyone who looks at a situation realistically and from different perspectives can no longer get upset, as before.

Case Example 5 Follow-Up: Infidelity

It is understandable when Ms. U. is terribly upset, cries, swears, throws objects around, and has the impulse to kill her ex-fiancé and friend. She might be full of anger. However, does that help her to get out of it? Probably not. She could say to herself, in an internal dialogue: "Don't freak out, stay cool, keep your self-control and stay self-confident." She remembers that her ex-fiancé was by no means always a superhero in bed. Another question is how she would like to come across on TV if she was secretly filmed. The story is so grotesque that even that is imaginable. And when she puts herself in the shoes of her ex-fiancé and friend, then pity can almost arise because she can see that they have so little self-control.

> **Case Example 6 Follow-Up: Club**
>
> Mr. V. is undoubtedly a man who also cares about his social position and the effect it has on others. Otherwise, the position of club president would not be so important to him. Now that he has been voted out, everyone is waiting to see how he behaves. You can undoubtedly achieve more with a calm behavior than with a lack of self-control. It makes little sense to indulge in emotional outbursts and show everyone how hurt and ashamed you are. To be confident in this case would mean taking the election result calmly, congratulating the new chairman, even giving a little speech, and wishing him all the best, thanking the club members for their many years of support, pointing out how much work and responsibility one is now free of, etc. Anger does not help, and other emotions are needed: gratitude, joy, self-confidence, relief, etc.

> **Tipp**
>
> When solving a difficult problem, it is wise to stay calm and not to loose your sense of humor.

4.14 Long-Term Perspective – What Matters Is the Future

People often behave as the moment requires, and that may or may not work out very well. It can produce wonderful results in the short term. However, it can turn out to be very stupid in the long run. The ancient Greeks spoke of a Pyrrhic victory, where you win a battle and lose the war. Behavior guided by a long-term perspective is not always easy. Everyone knows this from the challenges of healthy eating or exercise. The food tastes so good, and in the long run, the weight increases. Another familiar example of the difference between short-term and long-term consequences is what can happen in school. A student who thinks in the short term may avoid going to school in the cold in the morning, because they do not want to face a difficult math test. It is in that moment better to stay at home. In the long term, however, it is better to graduate. That is why the student has to get up despite the current adversity. In psychology, overcoming short-term negative states in favor of behavior control based on long-term positive goals is called *self-control*. My partner may be absolutely annoying right now, and I would like to punch them. I could immediately calm down after that. But does this act also stabilize and help my partnership in the future?

A long-term perspective can be promoted by looking back from the future. Just imagine that one day you have to tell your grandchildren your life story. How would you then like to describe the current situation: "I lost my temper and attacked my boss with my fists?" You would probably be better off, if you could truthfully say: "I was terribly angry, but I controlled myself, and then talked to my boss in a particularly friendly manner and in the end I even got a better job."

> **Case Example 5 Follow-Up: Infidelity**
>
> It might be understandable if Ms. U. physically attacked her ex-fiancé and her friend; she could scream in front of all of the guests and make a scene, she could withdraw herself, or even think of suicide. Do any of those help manage the problem, and what would be the result in the future? Should a failed wedding lead to a miserable life filled with grief, anger, and vengeance? One "stupid guy" should not be allowed to mess up her whole life! From a long-term perspective, it would even be conceivable that she will thank her friend, as a last-minute loyalty tester, so to speak. If she had married this man, she could have bet that he would continue to be unfaithful. Her friend saved her from a worse outcome. It was a blessing in disguise!

> **Case Example 6 Follow-Up: Club**
>
> Mr. V. can act from a short-term or from a long-term perspective. In the short term, he could publicly disagree with the election result, curse the voters, show himself offended, etc. The result would probably be that the club members would see themselves strengthened in their belief that they were right in not reelecting him. A long-term perspective gives you completely different ideas. You are a good loser and thus keep open all possibilities to run again in the next election. You behave in such a way that you remain a valued club member and can continue to participate in all club activities. You can also think beyond the club. What are your new freedoms? Are there other activities in which your wife and children could participate? What is best for your health in the long-term? From a long-term perspective, you could be a little creative and first of all dream about the many possibilities the future holds.

> **Tipp**
>
> When solving a difficult problem, it is wise to always think about long-term consequences.

4.15 Bringing the Past to a Close and Forgiving – Over Is Over

What has happened cannot be undone. After a death, nobody brings the person back to life, infidelity cannot be undone, and an insult cannot be magically reversed into a beautiful experience. The good thing is that a lot of that will now belong to the past. Coming to terms with the past means learning from the past and then letting it rest. Imagine that one partner has cheated, and the other one then says that they want to announce an annual commemorative day, and they erect a monument to infidelity in their living room. A bigger nonsense is probably not imaginable. This turns the previous problem into a permanent problem for both partners. That certainly does not help bring peace and a good future, nor does it help your own well-being. Both of you will continue to suffer, and will suffer even more because you cannot let the past rest. An injustice you have experienced does not have to do you extra harm by your continuously thinking back to it with negative emotions. It cannot be undone anymore. So you have to accept the past and let it rest. This does not mean downplaying what happened, but to free yourself from memories and revenge fantasies. Always reminding yourself of the past does not undo the injustice, but leads to ongoing difficulties and impaired personal well-being.

Philosophers and theologians have known this for a long time. Psychologists have empirically found out that the most important method of coming to terms with the past is forgiveness. According to forgiveness psychology, there are several levels to be distinguished:

- Justification: No one is to blame for the circumstances; there is no reason for any accusations to be made.
- Understanding: Even if something bad has happened, you can understand how it came about; it could have been different, but there is no reason for anger.
- Forgiveness: No matter what happened, you let things rest. Stop feeling resentment or a desire for revenge. Forgiveness only takes place inside yourself.
- Condoning: You tell the guilty person that you have forgiven them. This is a social act. It does not mean you have to forego punishment.
- Reconciliation: You go back to your starting point.
- Pardoning: You do not feel the for need any punishment or payback.
- Forgetting: You detach yourself from your memories.

This means that forgiveness is at its core something very selfish. You focus on yourself and bring an end to what has happened to you. When a partner has been unfaithful, to forgive means to put an end to it, to get a clean break and not to look back, and to turn to the future. You do not have to tell the unfaithful person that you no longer care, you can still get as much money out of the divorce proceedings as possible, and you do not have to keep on living with them. If you are no longer interested in anything, you may even end up forgetting everything, even if that is likely to be the exception.

> **Case Example 5 Follow-Up: Infidelity**
>
> The fact that a partner has cheated on you cannot be undone, as much as Ms. U. may wish it in her own case. To ruin your life for the coming years by constantly thinking about it and mulling over the past does not change what happened. Rather, in the long run, it poisons your own experience. That would be a double punishment. Ms. U.'s ex-fiancé is gone, and so is her good sleep and ever being in a good mood.
>
> If Ms. U. wants to feel good again, she must forgive. That means thinking that the ex-boyfriend was someone not worth marrying, that it was a stupid situation, and that she would have liked to not have this experience, that she will take a closer look at the next man she is attracted to, that she will let past matters rest, will not waste any more thought on the incident, and therefore no longer harbor any anger or feelings of any desire for revenge. Just forget it!
>
> Instead, there is the question of the future. Ms. U. is still young. There are other men and certainly better ones out there. It is reasonable to look for one. That should be possible.

> **Case Example 6 Follow-Up: Club**
>
> If Mr. V. wants to stay in his beloved club, he will see the new chairman every time he goes there. He is constantly reminded. Forgiveness means to put an end to his mental injuries and his urge for retaliation and revenge. Forgiveness psychology specifies that forgiveness is essentially also an act of will. Mr. V. must therefore make a conscious decision to forgive. He must say to himself: "I no longer want to fight back but will make peace with the situation. I want to accept that the other person has won, and I don't want to blame them for that."

> **Tipp**
>
> When solving a difficult problem, it is wise not to let the past block future opportunities.

4.16 Uncertainty Tolerance – Accepting What the Future Will Bring

Life is uncertain and unpredictable. Nobody can tell if they will still be alive the next day. In half of cases, those who marry must expect their marriage to break up. Being able to accept that you never know what is coming is called *uncertainty tolerance*.

Many people believe or expect that they will have everything under control. Car accidents only happen to others. I drive carefully. Others do not even think ahead. They walk across the street without looking left or right. Others may have had bad experiences and can no longer turn a blind eye to the dangers. You no longer drive a car, unlike the many other drivers who populate the street.

Uncertainty tolerance means to accept that "predictions are difficult, especially when they concern the future," as a well-known proverb goes. It also means starting with a minimum of optimism despite all the uncertainties. Someone whose relationship has once failed, can still get involved with a new partner. Even if it is again not certain how it will turn out. In fact, there is actually a chance that it will be better next time. In this respect, tolerance of uncertainty also has its advantages. Anyone who is aware that relationships can fail will therefore do more to ensure that it does not happen, right from the beginning.

> **Case Example 5 Follow-Up: Infidelity**
>
> Ms. U. could adopt the idea that men can not be trusted and that any new relationship should therefore be avoided. It is surely uncertain whether the next partner will be absolutely loyal. But, if she withdraws herself, she may miss the best relationship of her life. Actually, it does not really matter what she does. There are many ways to fail or to be happy. Who knows what is coming next? You have to behave in one way or another, whether you want to or not, and thus accept the respective risks. So all that remains is to march forward happily with a bit of optimism. Ms. U. could therefore go on with her life as before. What if she meets another man? Then she is now more experienced and wiser than before and will already know what has to be done so that it goes better this time – though, of course, no one can give her a guarantee. Still, it is worth a try.

> **Case Example 6 Follow-Up: Club**
>
> The voting out of office of Mr. V. is a classic example of the fact that you can never be sure what is coming next. If he had taken that into account from day

one, would he have become the club's chairman? Probably yes. Perhaps the knowledge of the unpredictability of life would have helped him to adjust to the fact that someone else might be voted in. He would not have been so surprised at being voted out. Perhaps he would not have been voted out, because he would have been aware that there is always a chance of not being re-elected, so he would have taken preventive measures. Maybe instead of arrogant self-assurance, a little more fighting spirit would have emerged.

Tipp

If you want to solve a difficult problem, it is wise to approach things courageously and also to accept failure when it comes.

4.17 Difficult Problems and Simple Solutions

We have now presented a number of wisdom strategies that are helpful when someone is facing difficult problems. The various elements are connected. If I give a clear and realistic description of the facts and leave nothing out, then I will stumble on what others actually think. If I have made a change of perspective, this also helps to classify my own position better, which in turn is good for getting one's emotions under control. If I can deal with my emotions, which is the most difficult thing, then I can take forward-looking steps that are beneficial to me. It is wise not to neglect any of the 13 dimensions of wisdom and wisdom competencies. In summary, it is about comprehensive problem-solving skills.

All of this is needed to cope with difficult moments in life, such as marriage breakdown, job dismissal, illness, and death. But it is also needed in everyday life, as the simple example of what orange juice to purchase shows (see Section 4.1: Wisdom as a Problem-Solving Ability). Without being aware of it, we recapitulate what we know when shopping for orange juice. We endure the uncertainty of not knowing whether the two cartons contain juice that is any different. We weigh values against each other – for example, money against health – and consider what the long-term result could be if you bought the expensive or the cheap juice. You think about the current situation – that is, who is the juice for, and how much money do you have in your wallet? You may get annoyed that your partner insists on the expensive juice, even though you think it is a waste of money.

So wisdom is a competence everyone is capable of, just as everybody has social competence and self-confidence. However, there are people who have a high level of social skills, and others who tend to have limited social skills.

And if it is necessary, you can learn and be trained in social skills. It is the same with wisdom competencies. There are people with more or less wisdom. People who are stuck in difficult problems should try to activate their wisdom skills and, if necessary, improve them. Anyone who notices that they are offensive to other people should consider improving their social skills. Those who can no longer get rid of problems should work on their wisdom skills.

Wisdom research gives some interesting suggestions. Wisdom is more important for one's own well-being and life satisfaction than money and social status are. On average, wisdom increases slightly with age but unfortunately, not necessarily. There are young people with high wisdom skills, and older people who have gained very little wisdom. But it is also comforting that wisdom has nothing to do with formal schooling. There are professors who are "wisdom stupid," while someone who only finished elementary school could be extremely wise. So there is hope for everyone.

5
What Is Psychotherapy?

If you cannot get out of your embitterment on your own, psychotherapy can help. The following describes the principles according to which psychotherapists help those affected by embitterment to free themselves from it.

5.1 How Do I Find a Therapist?

Psychotherapy is a treatment method that is paid for by health insurance in many countries. *Psychotherapists* are doctors or psychologists with additional training in psychotherapy. Many health insurance companies check the training of psychotherapists and request a case report before the start of therapy, which is checked by another therapist for appropriateness. You should be careful to avoid putting yourself in the hands of people who are not licensed professional therapists, as psychotherapy can cause harm.

The first step to finding a psychotherapist is to see a family doctor or primary care physician. General practitioners and in particular psychiatrists have a lot of experience with people who suffer from mental disorders. The family doctor can therefore first check how the problem at hand presents itself from a professional perspective and then refer you to a psychotherapist or psychiatrist. Is it really about embitterment, depression, or something else? Depending on the result of this evaluation, the treatment can, of course, be very different. The family doctor will know what to do and give advice. If the family doctor is involved in the treatment from the start, this also has the advantage of having someone who is available in crisis situations. GPs see a lot of people in distress or suffering from mental disorders and have a lot of experience in this regard.

Another reason to involve the family doctor right from the start is that psychotherapy is mostly limited regarding the number of sessions. If those end, then many patients may still need support and guidance.

If the family doctor sees an embitterment problem in need of treatment, they can give a recommendation as to which therapist should be approached. The family doctor often knows which psychotherapists work in their area. A psychotherapist should not be too far away, as you sometimes have to go there every week for a longer time. If necessary, the family doctor can also contact the psychotherapist directly, which makes it easier to get an appointment.

5.2 What Do Psychotherapists Do?

In the interactions with the patient, a psychotherapist will try to (a) analyze the problem in detail, (b) work out what is particularly bad, (c) consider what can be done to clarify the matter, (d) trace what prevents you from solving the problem, (e) illuminate which previous experiences are important, (f) work out how you can develop new perspectives and come to terms with the past, and (g) help you develop and improve new problem-solving skills. This is a full program and covers many of the already described wisdom strategies.

The methods used in psychotherapy are based on scientific evidence and results from clinical studies. There are psychotherapeutic approaches such as cognitive behavior therapy, psychodynamic psychotherapy, and systemic psychotherapy. Nevertheless, all psychotherapists will follow individualized treatment concepts tailored to the individual patient and their problems.

One of these scientifically tested psychotherapeutic methods to overcome embitterment is *wisdom therapy* (see Chapter 4: Wisdom). This was developed for the treatment of *posttraumatic embitterment disorder*. As the name of the therapy implies, it is directed to improving wisdom skills, in this case, to counteract embitterment. This is about improving the ability to solve complex problems, helping the person affected out of their current problems, lowering psychological stress, and improving skills to withstand future critical life events.

6
What Can Relatives Do?

We have described in detail that embitterment is associated with cynicism, withdrawal, aggression, and also viciousness toward the environment. Relatives, friends, family members, or partners of embittered people often suffer from this. That means embitterment is an emotion with a significant social impact.

The bad mood of a loved one or the rejection of benevolent help is sometimes just as burdensome for those around the embittered person as for those directly affected. Those bystanders are also the ones to see the drama, the abnormality, and the absurdity in all its glory. They want to help and are rejected, sometimes even pushed back. Often, the people surrounding the embittered person are the first ones to seek help, rather than the embittered person themself.

When relatives want to change the situation, they try to talk to those affected. This often leads to additional misunderstandings. The advice to let go of what has happened is understood as if it showed that others can not understand what happened, or they even ally themselves with the aggressor. It quickly becomes clear that the problem cannot simply be talked away and that one's own expertise quickly reaches its limits. The consequence can be *reactance* on the part of the person's social surroundings, who may say things like "If you don't want to be helped, then get lost and do what you want!" The person concerned then feels vindicated in their perception that they are all alone.

What advice is helpful for relatives? Here, too, the aforementioned wisdom competencies should be remembered (see Chapter 4: Wisdom). A change of perspective and emotional empathy can help to understand the terrible state of the embittered person. Value relativism can make it understandable what it was that affected the person concerned in such a way that it was not a triviality, but rather led to their entire understanding of themself and the world being called into question. Self-relativization can help to accept that you cannot change anything in the situation, but can only continue to stand by and not leave them alone, even if they insult, reject, or attack you in their doggedness. Whoever can manage that deserves respect. Parents manage this again and again, partners and children less often, friends are usually gone quite quickly.

The second piece of advice is to signal understanding rather than to try to discuss. Discussions lead nowhere. Relatives should not get impatient if they hear the same arguments and statements over and over again. A change of perspective enables relatives to convey to the embittered person that you understand them, that you can understand what drives them, and that you are listening. You do not have to be of the same opinion. This is similar to your partner stating that you destroy the environment as you eat a steak. You can understand that and accept their concerns. However, you are allowed to have a different opinion and enjoy your steak.

The next step is to empathize with the suffering of the embittered person. Embitterment hurts. You can see that from the outside. Someone who is happy and satisfied looks different. By using empathy, you may ask the person whether they can do anything to improve their misery. If something bad has happened to you, you do not deserve to feel badly too. Who could give you advice and help?

7
Further Reading

Linden, M., & Arnold, C. P. (2021). Embitterment and posttraumatic embitterment disorder (PTED): An old, frequent, and still underrecognized problem. *Psychotherapy and Psychosomatics, 90*, 73–80.

Linden, M., & Maercker, A. (2011). *Embitterment: Societal, psychological, and clinical perspectives.* Springer.

Linden, M., Rotter, M., Baumann, K., & Lieberei, B. (2006). *The posttraumatic embitterment disorder: Definition, evidence, diagnosis, treatment.* Hogrefe.

Linden, M., & Rutkowski, K. (2013). *Hurting memories and beneficial forgetting: Posttraumatic stress disorders, biographical developments, and social conflicts.* Newnes.

8
Embitterment Checklist

Everyone has known embitterment and will have experienced this emotion more or less intensely.

Are you (or someone you know) embittered?

Have you recently experienced a severe and negative life event about which you would say any or all of the following?

	Disagree	Somewhat agree	Strongly agree
The event hurt my feelings and caused considerable embitterment.	0	1	2
It was something that I see as very unjust and unfair.	0	1	2
About which I have to think over and over again.	0	1	2
That causes me to be extremely upset when I am reminded of it.	0	1	2
That triggers in me the harboring of thoughts of revenge, and on basis of which I am entitled to get compensation.	0	1	2
For which I blame and am angry with myself.	0	1	2
That causes me to avoid certain places or persons so as to not be reminded of them.	0	1	2
That has led to a noticeable and persistent negative change in my mental well-being.	0	1	2
That has made me unable to pursue occupational and/or family activities as before.	0	1	2

If you scored 9 points or more, then you have not yet mastered the severe life event adequately and should do something about it – that is, discuss the matter with someone you trust or, if necessary, consult a therapist. The lower your score, the better you have managed what happened.

This page may be reproduced by the purchaser for personal/clinical use.
From: C. P. Arnold and M. Linden: *How to Overcome Embitterment With Wisdom*
© 2023 Hogrefe Publishing

9
Important Addresses

USA

National Suicide Prevention Lifeline
Telephone: 1-800-273-8255 (English) or 1-888-628-9454 (Spanish)
Emergency referrals to social and community services: 211

UK & Ireland

Samaritans UK & Ireland
116 123

Shout (Text service only in UK)
Text SHOUT on 85258

Notes on Supplementary Materials

The following materials for your book can be downloaded free of charge once you register on our website:

Appendix 1: Embitterment checklist

How to proceed:

1. Create a user account (or, if you have already one, please log in)

For customers from the USA, Canada, and the rest of the world: hgf.io/login-us

For European customers: hgf.io/login-eu

2. Download your supplementary materials
Go to **My supplementary materials** in your account dashboard and enter the code below. You will automatically be redirected to the download area, where you can access and download the supplementary materials.

Code: **B-750LRS**

To make sure you have permanent direct access to all the materials, we recommend that you download them and save them on your computer.

Peer commentaries

Anyone who is struggling with feelings of embitterment will find this book to be a wonderfully accessible description of the psychological state of embitterment that is replete with stories of the dangers and consequences of this emotional response. The exercises and examples the book presents will help readers develop a deeper understanding of their responses and to consider strategies for coping better with this challenging and complex emotional state.

Heidi M. Levitt, PhD, Department of Psychology, University of Massachusetts, Boston, MA, USA

In their book *How to Overcome Embitterment by Wisdom*, Christopher Arnold and Michael Linden provide a comprehensive description, using real-life case examples, of an emotion known to us all – embitterment. This book is a powerful lever to foster learning about embitterment: how it arises, what triggers it, its consequences, and when you should seek professional help. The expert authors also highlight the importance of "wisdom," a skill that we can all cultivate to "escape" from embitterment. The authors have fused together findings from their clinical practice and research with the real world to produce an innovative book that is highly accessible to everyone. I am sure that not only people suffering from embitterment but also researchers and clinicians working in this field will benefit greatly from reading it.

Evie Michailidis, PhD, Psychology Department, University of Cyprus, Cyprus

Help clients overcome feelings of embitterment

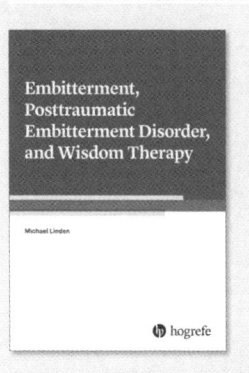

Michael Linden

Embitterment, Posttraumatic Embitterment Disorder, and Wisdom Therapy

2023, viii + 106 pp.
US $29.80 / € 25.95
ISBN 978-0-88937-612-0
Also available as eBook

Feelings of embitterment and posttraumatic embitterment disorder are common in our society and result from reactions to injustices, humiliation, and breaches of trust. They can lead to significant suffering in those affected and to those around them. The aggressiveness of this client group, as well as their rejection of help, is challenging for practitioners and makes treatment complex. Help is at hand with this practical evidence-based guide that provides models for the development and continuation of such embitterment states. The reader is guided through the state-of-the-art treatment approaches for embitterment disorder: cognitive behavior therapy with wisdom strategies.

Teach your clients how to process their internalized feelings of hurt and humiliation so they can reconcile themselves with the events that triggered these difficult and long-lasting states. The book is full of practice-oriented tips to help clients actively gain closure with the past and enable a new orientation towards the future. One method to reach this goal is the reevaluation of the critical events and their consequences. Wisdom therapy provides various tools for this. Tips are also given on the social, medical, and legal aspects associated with this disorder.

A companion book for clients is also available: *How to Overcome Embitterment With Wisdom*

www.hogrefe.com

hogrefe

How to provide culturally sensitive care for clients with PTSD

Andreas Maercker / Eva Heim / Laurence J. Kirmayer

Cultural Clinical Psychology and PTSD

2019, x + 236 pp.
US $62.00 / € 49.95
ISBN 978-0-88937-497-3
Also available as eBook

This book, written and edited by leading experts from around the world, looks critically at how culture impacts on the way posttraumatic stress disorder (PTSD) and related disorders are diagnosed and treated. There have been important advances in clinical treatment and research on PTSD, partly as a result of researchers and clinicians increasingly taking into account how "culture matters."

For mental health professionals who strive to respond to the needs of people from diverse cultures who have experienced traumatic events, this book is invaluable. It presents recent research and practical approaches on key topics, including:

- How culture shapes mental health and recovery
- How to integrate culture and context into PTSD theory
- How trauma-related distress is experienced and expressed in different cultures, reflecting local values, idioms, and metaphors
- How to integrate cultural dimensions into psychological interventions.

Providing new theoretical insights as well as practical advice, it will be of interest to clinical psychologists, psychiatrists, and other health professionals, as well as researchers and students engaged with mental health issues, both globally and locally.

www.hogrefe.com

hogrefe